Introduction to the Bible

Introduction to the Bible

A Catholic Guide to Studying Scripture

Stephen J. Binz

LITURGICAL PRESS
Collegeville, Minnesota

www.litpress.org

Cover design by Ann Blattner.

Nihil Obstat: Rev. Robert C. Harren, J.C.L., Censor deputatus.
Imprimatur: ✛ Most Rev. John F. Kinney, J.C.D., D.D.,
           Bishop of St. Cloud, August 1, 2006.

		4	5	6	7	8	9

Library of Congress Cataloging-in-Publication Data

Binz, Stephen J., 1955–
    Introduction to the Bible : a Catholic guide to studying Scripure /
Stephen J. Binz.
        p.   cm.
    ISBN-13: 978-0-8146-1700-7
    ISBN-10: 0-8146-1700-X
    1. Bible—Study and teaching.   2. Catholic Church—Doctrines.   I. Title.
BS600.3.B52 2007
220.6'1—dc22

                                                        2006020573

Contents

Preface

During the generations of my parents and grandparents, Catholicism and personal Bible reading were not normally associated with one another. Sure, the Bible was revered; its presence evoked an awe associated with divine holiness. Most Catholic homes had a family Bible, usually with gilt-edged pages and filled with pages of religious art. More often than not, the Bible held an honored place in the family living room, and contained the baptism, marriage, and funeral records of the family. Catholics knew that there were people in the church who studied the Bible; surely the parish pastor had read and understood some of it. But rarely would a lay Catholic ever break the spine of the family Bible and actually begin to read.

Our Protestant neighbors were the ones who read the Bible. In fact, the Bible was what their faith was about. But Catholics, we had the Mass, the sacraments, the catechism, personal devotions, Mary, and the saints. These were the ways we experienced the presence of God and learned about our religion. What more could we need?

There are lots of historical reasons for this Catholic state of affairs in the middle of the twentieth century. The church had an exaggerated fear of private interpretation of the Bible. Couldn't reading one's own Bible lead to all sorts of false understanding? Better to let the church teach us what we needed to know.

But all this started rapidly changing in the 1960s. One of the most significant changes of the Second Vatican Council was the church's direct encouragement for Catholics to rediscover the Bible. The reformed liturgy contained a wide selection of readings from both the Old and New

Testaments. The church placed Sacred Scripture at the heart of liturgical preaching, religious education, and personal devotions. Catholics began to be exposed to biblical texts that they had never heard, and many started reading the Bible like never before.

Unlike the Catholicism of my parents and grandparents, my life as a Catholic has been infused with this biblical renewal in the church. When I was still a teenager, I heard about a group of priests, sisters, and lay-people in my city who were forming a Catholic method of Bible study called Little Rock Scripture Study. They were gathering people in parishes to study the Bible and discuss it together. I had no idea in the mid-70s that this fledgling movement in my town of Little Rock would grow so rapidly and be so influential in determining the direction of my life.

As I attended a Catholic university in another city, I realized what a fascinating experience studying the Bible could be. After taking my first undergraduate classes in the Bible, I was hooked. I knew that this sacred book would become critically important as my life progressed. Scripture became the foundation of my personal and professional life as I continued to pursue advanced degrees in biblical study and to teach and write in this growing field.

Catholic biblical scholarship had been advancing in the academic world since Pope Pius XII gave it his highest endorsement in a 1943 encyclical called *Divino Afflante Spiritu*. The Jesuit institute where I studied was one of the global centers of Catholic scholarship that had prepared the way for the biblical renewal that was bursting out in the church. During this time, Catholic biblical scholars, who had been quietly doing their work in "ivory towers" for decades, began to lecture and publish widely on the Bible. It didn't take long for Catholic scholars to catch up with their more advanced Protestant colleagues. With the endorsement of the Pope and bishops, rooted in solid scholarship, and impelled by a spirit of renewal that was palpably alive in the church, the Catholic biblical renewal was underway.

In the decades after Vatican II, Catholic parishes could not keep pace with the desire of Catholics to learn about the Bible. We were reclaiming our legacy and resurrecting a lost part of our heritage. Little Rock Scripture Study grew rapidly, throughout the United States and into many other countries. Soon many scholars were writing materials for use by lay Catholics, and most Catholic publishers were producing a variety of materials to help make reading the Bible an essential part of Catholic life.

Today, in the twenty-first century, this vision of bringing Catholic Bible study to the masses continues to flourish. Little Rock Scripture Study and other Bible study programs continue to grow worldwide. The revolutionary freshness of the Council reforms has worn off, but the church is in a new epoch. Our recent popes, John Paul II and Benedict XVI, have called our era a new springtime for the church, and they have urged us to undertake a new evangelization. Our bishops have called us to study our faith with new vigor and make adult faith formation a high priority. More than ever before, Catholic Bible study is essential for the ongoing renewal of our church.

Though studying the Bible still seems fairly new for many Catholics, in fact, the Bible has always been at the heart of the church. It is the family album of the people of God. As we look to the future, there is no better way for the church to be continually renewed than through the Sacred Scriptures. As more and more Catholics begin studying the Bible and putting it at the center of their lives of prayer, we will begin to find our way as a church in this new era. With catechesis and spirituality rooted in the Bible, we will understand ever more clearly the direction God wants us to take.

I am grateful for the people in my life who have taught me the Bible and who have been partners with me in the work of offering Bible materials to the people of God. I am grateful for the academic fellowship I enjoy with members of the Catholic Biblical Association of America. I am particularly thankful to the staff of Little Rock Scripture Study and its director, Cackie Upchurch, for inviting me to write this book. I am also thankful to Peter Dwyer and the team at Liturgical Press for their faithful partnership with the Diocese of Little Rock in the service of Catholic Bible Study and for directing the publication of this book. This ministry of God's word is the most rewarding life I could imagine, and I am so grateful that my life was caught up in the biblical renewal of the Catholic Church.

Whether you are a first-time reader of the Bible or have been studying Scripture for a while, you have picked up this book because you want to be a part of this rekindling of biblical fervor in the church. I want to encourage and assure you that putting the Bible at the heart of your life in Christ can indeed transform you. When you make reflective reading and study of the Bible a part of your daily life, you will notice changes within yourself that will deepen your spirituality and lead you in a direction you sincerely desire. As you reflect on this ancient, inspired literature of God's family, you will become ever more fully a child of God and enter more deeply into a personal relationship with Jesus the Lord. This book is only an invitation to that adventure of a lifetime. I pray that it will lead you to a renewed and committed life in Christ's church.

CHAPTER ONE

The Bible As God's Self-Revelation

Our God is not a God who is concealed from us, obscurely hidden in eternity and unavailable. Our God is present to us, dynamically alive, communicating with creation, and entering into a relationship with humanity. God reveals the divine presence to us in many ways: through the beauty and wonders of creation, through the goodness of people, through quiet reflection and prayer, through the inner voice of our conscience, and through the many experiences of human life in the world.

We discern something of God's reality in each of these ways when we sense an ultimate meaning within our experiences and perceive the deeper reality behind life's events. When nature, friendship, love, struggle, contemplation, or joy leads us to understand a significance or purpose beyond the surface of things, we experience something of God's personal existence.

God has made his presence known in more specific ways in human history: liberating people from bondage, gathering them into a special community, guiding them to worship and practice justice, and offering them a life with meaning and hope. Above all, God has revealed the divine presence to humanity through the person and life of Jesus Christ. And God continues to reveal himself in Jesus' abiding presence, through the Holy Spirit alive in the church.

This self-revelation of God and people's response to it throughout history is called salvation history. God has been guiding creation through the centuries to experience the fullness of life, and God continues to reveal himself today. We are each a part of this ongoing history of salvation. God continually calls people to a deeper and fuller understanding of—and a more personal response to—this divine revelation.

The Second Vatican Council, in its document on Divine Revelation, expressed it this way:

> By this revelation, then, the invisible God, from the fullness of his love, addresses men as his friends, and moves among them, in order to invite and receive them into his own company. (*Dogmatic Constitution on Divine Revelation*, 2; can also be found in the *Catechism of the Catholic Church*, 142)[1]

The Bible is a primary and honored expression of this self-revelation of God. It is about how God shows the divine presence through words and deeds in history. The Bible shows us that God is not as interested in giving us information about himself as God desires to show himself to us personally. Because the Bible is a means of God's self-revelation to us, we can come to know God more fully through the words of the Bible.

God Entered into an Ongoing Covenant

God discloses the divine presence to us in order to enter into a personal relationship with us. This relationship that God has entered with us is called the covenant. The whole Bible is the expression of this covenant, this ongoing relationship that God began with people centuries ago and continues now in our own lives. This covenant relationship is a two-way street: God reveals, and God's people respond.

God entered into covenant with the Hebrew people and disclosed his presence to them. God chose them by a free act of love to be his own people, and they responded with faith and love. Through the covenant God promised many blessings to his people, and they agreed to certain responsibilities that flow from that relationship. God first revealed this relationship to Abraham, promising countless descendants, a special land, and abundant blessings. Abraham's response changed his life and changed human history. Through Moses, God made the people of Israel his own people and revealed the terms of their relationship. The covenant was renewed many times throughout history through the kings and

---

[1] Recognizing that many Catholics do not have access to the documents of the Second Vatican Council, but do have the *Catechism* more readily at hand, I list both sources for the reader's convenience.

prophets of Israel. Finally, God entered into the fullest relationship possible with his people by sending his Son. The life, death, and resurrection of Jesus ratified the new covenant, the completed and fullest relationship between God and humanity.

Since we can speak about God only in human words, using images and symbols rooted in our own experience, the Bible uses a variety of analogies to express this unique relationship. God is Father, and we are his children; God is the bridegroom, and we are his bride; God is the shepherd and we are the flock; God is the mother eagle caring for her young and teaching them to fly. You will find many more images of God and his relationship with us throughout the books of the Bible.

God first set his heart on the people of Israel and chose them to be his own simply because of love (Deut 7:6-8). They were neither powerful, numerous, nor virtuous as a people; they possessed no particular qualities that would draw God to them. God's choice of them was pure gift. Today, God's saving desire extends to all the people of the earth, but God actualizes this divine saving mission one person at a time. As people who have been baptized into Christ's church and called to study Sacred Scripture, we have been freely given the grace of sharing in God's life.

The Bible is the literature of the covenant, and it invites us to enter into the covenant ourselves. Through the Bible, not only do we learn about God's relationship with people of ancient times, but we become a part of that covenant. By entering into relationship with God, we become a part of this ongoing history of salvation, which gives meaning, purpose, and hope to our lives.

The Old Testament

The Bible expresses God's desire to bring salvation to the entire world. In preparation for this, God chose to reveal himself to a particular people as the one, true, and living God. Through covenant, God gradually disclosed his promises to redeem and sanctify all of humanity. Israel learned of God's will for creation through their history as God's chosen people. Through the prophets, kings, and priests of Israel, God disclosed his saving will and merciful love.

The inspired writers of the Old Testament recounted and explained God's saving plan as it gradually unfolded. Their writings appear as the living word of God in the books of the Old Testament. The word "old" is a term of honor and respect for these ancient Scriptures. It does not at all mean that these books are obsolete or outdated. In fact, the covenant God made with Israel has not and cannot be annulled. As Paul wrote about God's election of the Jewish people, "The gifts and the call of God are irrevocable" (Rom 11:29). The Old Testament writings retain a lasting value and are critically important for understanding God's saving work. As Paul continues, "Whatever was written previously was written for our instruction, that by endurance and by the encouragement of the scriptures we might have hope" (Rom 15:4).

Sometimes Christians beginning to study the Bible place a lesser value on the Old Testament because they consider these books to be less significant than the New Testament books. But for Christians, both the Old Testament and the New Testament together express the inspired word of God. The Old Testament books are essential for understanding the history of salvation, and we cannot properly understand the New without understanding the Old. Only in the light of the Old Testament can the Christian comprehend the significance of the life, death, and glorification of Jesus.

The New Testament

Through countless quotations and references, the New Testament writers bring the Old Testament into their Scriptures. Clearly these writers honor the Old Testament as the inspired word of God and demonstrate that those ancient texts attain and display their full meaning in the New Testament. God's saving plan, manifested in the Old, comes to fulfillment in the New. In this way, the whole Bible demonstrates the complete saving will of God for the world as it came to its fullness in Jesus Christ.

In the fifth century, St. Augustine expressed the church's belief in the unity of the whole Bible: "The New Testament lies hidden in the Old, and the Old becomes clear in the New." Since God is the inspirer and primary author of both testaments, they fit together in a wonderful unity of promise and fulfillment. In coming to appreciate the value of each part of God's word in Sacred Scripture, we can grow to understand God's total plan as it was gradually revealed through the history of Israel and Christ's church. From Genesis to Revelation, the biblical books reveal the single, overarching plan of God to share his life with the world.

"When the fullness of time had come" (Gal 4:4), God sent his Son among us as the culmination of his saving will. John's gospel expressed this climactic moment in the history of salvation with this magnificent verse:

> And the Word became flesh
> and made his dwelling among us,
> and we saw his glory,

the glory of the Father's only Son,
full of grace and truth. (John 1:14)

Jesus established God's kingdom in the world, revealed God's unfathomable love through his death and resurrection, and promised his Spirit to establish his church to continue his saving work. The writings of the New Testament stand as God's inspired witness to these astonishing realities.

Roadblocks to Reading the Bible

How can I ever hope to read such a huge book? How can I understand the Bible when even scholars can't understand it? How can I interpret the Bible when it is the cause of so much controversy and division? How can I understand the Bible that is written in such ancient language about events that happened so long ago? Why should I read the Bible when I seem to be getting along so well without it? These are the kinds of questions that people face when they consider the possibilities of studying the Bible. It is these kinds of uncertainties that sometimes prevent people from ever beginning to really read the Bible seriously. Let's try to respond to these major obstacles in order to understand the Bible better.

- *First, the Bible is not just one, overwhelmingly large book.* It is a small library of books. Every book of the Bible is different and unique. You do not need to read this library from beginning to end. By selecting from among the Bible's many different books and starting to read just one of them, the task becomes less overwhelming and even enjoyable.

- *Second, the Bible was never meant to be difficult.* It was written mostly by simple people, like fishermen, tentmakers, and shepherds. The biblical books were written about human experiences to show God's presence and guidance, and they were never intended to contain any mysterious language. The Bible expresses the faith of imperfect people very much like ourselves—people who believe that God cares about them and acts in their lives.

- *Third, the Bible was never intended to cause confusion and conflict between people.* Using the Bible to win arguments, prove our points, and show that others are wrong, is a serious abuse of the Bible. Approach these books with humility and wonder; they are the sacred literature of God's people.

- *Fourth, the Bible was written long ago, but that does not mean that we can't enter that ancient world and become a part of it.* There are many ways to bridge the gap between the ancient and modern world. We have translations today written in modern English. There are lots of tools, like maps, Bible dictionaries, and commentaries, that we can use to understand the ancient world better, thanks to modern scholarship.

- *Fifth, the Bible is not just an ancient book; it is also a contemporary book.* The basic needs and experiences of human beings who struggle and reach out to God are the same for all people in every time and place. The questions and struggles of our lives are the same as those of the people of the Bible, so the Bible responds to the realities of modern human existence.

- *Sixth, the Bible is the privileged place where we experience the communication of God to us.* If we seem to be getting along fine without reading the Bible, let's realize that the Scriptures can offer us so much more. Though God communicates with us in other ways, in the Bible we can be assured that we experience God's presence and truth calling us to a deeper encounter and understanding. St. Jerome said: "Ignorance of the Scriptures is ignorance of Christ." The Second Vatican Council spoke to the Church in our day when it proclaimed:

  > It follows that all the preaching of the Church, as indeed the entire Christian religion, should be nourished and ruled by sacred Scripture. In the sacred books the Father who is in heaven comes lovingly to meet his children, and talks with them. And such is the force and power of the Word of God that it can serve the Church as her support and vigor, and the children of the Church as strength for their faith, food for the soul, and a pure and lasting fount of spiritual life. (*Dogmatic Constitution on Divine Revelation*, 21; can also be partially found in the *Catechism of the Catholic Church*, 104)

CHAPTER TWO

The Word of God in Christian Life

From its beginnings, Christianity has been a sacramental religion. The church is the continuation of the healing, forgiving, nourishing presence of Christ calling us to new and deeper life. As the visible and tangible expression of Christ's continuing presence with us, the church is the sacrament of Christ's presence in the world. The church's seven sacraments are particular, climactic moments when Christ becomes present and active within the life of the community of faith.

Christ is also truly and uniquely present to his people in the words of Sacred Scripture. Through hearing and reading the Bible, we are brought into the transforming presence of Christ. This experience of the Lord in both word and sacrament is mirrored in the human experience of love. To truly know that we are loved, we need to both feel it and hear it. The sacraments are the touch of God's love; the Scriptures are the words of God's love. Together, God's word and the sacraments of his church offer a wondrous experience of God's ardent and personal love for us.

This unity of word and deed, Scripture and sacrament, is most fully expressed in the church's liturgy. The eucharistic liturgy is divided into two essential parts: the Liturgy of the Word and the Liturgy of the Eucharist. Both parts depend on one another for the fullness of Christian worship. The teachings of the church stress that both Scripture and Eucharist are the bread of life; both of them give spiritual nourishment to God's people:

> The Church has always venerated the divine Scriptures just as she venerated the Body of the Lord, in so far as she never ceases, particularly in the sacred liturgy, to partake of the bread of life and to offer it to the faithful from the one table of the Word of God and the Body of Christ. (*Dogmatic Constitution on Divine Revelation*, 21; can also be found in the *Catechism of the Catholic Church*, 103)

To give reverence to the presence of Christ in the Scriptures, the Second Vatican Council continued a practice that had begun at the Council of Ephesus in A.D. 431. On each day of the general sessions, the Scriptures were carried in procession and then enthroned as the center of focus. Through this ritual act, the church expressed its faith that Christ, living and present in his word, presided over the deliberations of the council. All the teachings of the church were to be guided by that living word of God.

In the liturgy of the church, we venerate the Scriptures as we venerate the Blessed Sacrament. Candles are often brought to the ambo where the Scriptures are proclaimed as well as to the altar. Incense is used as a sign of reverence to the presence of Christ in the gospels as well as at the sacrament of the altar. The ordained minister bows, crosses himself, and kisses the book—gestures communicating reverential awe toward the presence of Christ in the words of Sacred Scripture.

As Christ is present in the Scriptures proclaimed in liturgy, he is also present when we study and reflect on the Scriptures as part of our daily lives. When we read Scripture expecting that Jesus will speak to our lives and nourish us with his presence, we will be changed and renewed. Just as the sacraments affect our lives when we open ourselves to the grace shared with us in those sacred moments, the Scriptures also can transform us when we read them with an open heart.

When we read the Bible as the word of God, it becomes a personal communication to us. The word of God speaks to us here and now as individuals. Sometimes that word is a comforting and consoling word. At other times the word is severe and challenging. God's word can be both gentle and harsh, and the more we expect to be changed by it, the more God will move within us and share his life with us.

We can read the Bible as if it were an impersonal document. We can read those pages of paper and ink as a detached observer. But if we read the Bible as Sacred Scripture, as God's word, then we are impelled to personal involvement in the communication. The Bible challenges us to face God and to confront ourselves. If we read the Bible as the word of God, we cannot escape without a response.

Commitment to God's Word

Just as in any loving relationship, there are times in our communicating with God through the Scriptures that seem dry and unrewarding. There are also times of intense feelings and joy. In a relationship with God or with another person, both experiences are necessary parts of a committed life. When we become frustrated in reading the Bible and are tempted to just give up, we must realize that God is working within us in those difficult times as well.

Some parts of the Bible seem much more inspiring than others. Most of the time we can be nourished in faith more by the gospels than we can by the ritual laws recorded in Leviticus. Yet God can use any section of Scripture, even the most obscure, to speak to us. We need to be open to God speaking to us through even the most apparently unlikely passages.

We should not be afraid to admit that there is much in the Bible that we don't comprehend and that does not seem to speak to our situation. We need to approach God's word with humility, realizing that we don't have all the answers and that our understanding is limited. In our meekness, God works within us most boldly.

The best way to deepen our relationship with God in Christ is through daily reading of Scripture. If we read the Bible just when we feel like it, we limit the workings of God within us. If we read the Bible only when we are confused and troubled, we will only be able to share a partial aspect of God's life. In constancy, fidelity, and commitment, love grows. Daily communication, in good times and in bad, is the key to abiding love.

Every day of our lives we are given 1,440 minutes to live. If we spend fifteen of those minutes in reflectively encountering God's word to us, we will be gradually changed from the inside out. Those few special minutes will prepare us to hear God speak to us in other ways during the day. When we enter into the world of Scripture, then the word of God will enter into our world and into our lives in ways that we cannot even anticipate.

The Transforming Power of the Word of God

In our modern culture, words are cheap. The world around us is full of words, and most of them have little impact on us. We have become accustomed to tuning out most of the words we hear every day. We have learned to hear without really listening.

In the world of the Bible, however, the term "word" meant more than an expression of an idea. A word was an expression of the person, conveying the personality and authority of the one speaking. Words revealed a person's innermost self, and words spoken to another established a relationship with that person.

For this reason, the term "word of God" in biblical tradition describes God's self-revelation. God's word is unlike any other word. God's word is powerful, communicating the healing strength and saving authority of God. When we receive the word of God into our lives, we can expect to be changed.

God's word is the loving power that created the world: "By the word of the LORD the heavens were made" (Ps 33:6). Calling forth creation from nothing, that divine word continues to create and sustain all things in being. That all-powerful word is the primary cause of the world's ongoing existence. Unlike human words, the word of God is not fleeting, but is permanently valid: "Though the grass withers and the flower wilts, the word of our God stands forever" (Isa 40:8). In a world in which everything seems to be passing and increasingly disposable, we can trust that God's word is eternally valid as our source of unchanging truth.

So many of the words that we speak and hear throughout the day have no effect. But the utterance that goes forth from the mouth of God has an impact that is effective and that achieves its purpose. The prophet Isaiah speaks about God's word as a penetrating rain, watering the earth so that it may bear fruit:

> For just as from the heavens
>   the rain and the snow come down
> And do not return there
>   till they have watered the earth,
>   making it fertile and fruitful,
> Giving seed to him who sows
>   and bread to him who eats,
> So shall my word be
>   that goes forth from my mouth;
> It shall not return to me void,
>   but shall do my will,
>   achieving the end for which I sent it. (Isa 55:10-11)

When we allow the word of God to penetrate our lives, we can be assured that it will achieve God's purposes within us. Not only will God's word refresh us and help us to grow, it will cause us to bear the fruit that God intends for our lives.

God spoke his word to Israel's ancestors, then to Moses and all the prophets and, through them, to all of his people. The people of the biblical world experienced the voice of God speaking in their lives as an intense and penetrating fire, an announcement that shattered their conventional preconceptions and devastated their comfortable ideas. Jeremiah expressed the challenge of God's word: "Is not my word like fire, says the Lord, like a hammer shattering rocks?" (Jer 23:29). The author of Hebrews experienced this penetrating power of God's word and offered this reflection for his readers:

> Indeed, the word of God is living and effective, sharper than any two-edged sword, penetrating even between soul and spirit, joints and marrow, and able to discern reflections and thoughts of the heart. No creature is concealed from him, but everything is naked and exposed to the eyes of him to whom we must render an account. (Heb 4:12-13)

Like a piercing sword, the voice of God speaking penetrates into the deepest parts of our being. Because of the dynamic nature of God's word, it cannot be a superficial word that touches only the surface of our lives. When God reveals his own word to us, nothing in our lives can remain hidden. Everything about us is laid bare and nothing can be shielded from the searing, shattering, penetrating power of God.

When we allow God's word into our lives everything is subject to revision and transformation. Our path through life becomes illuminated by a guiding truth that shows us the way. We might be guided to follow a road we might not have chosen, to make choices that we couldn't have anticipated. The divine word that said, "Let there be light" (Gen 1:3), becomes a luminous beacon that guides our way through life's dark valleys. As the psalmist prayed to God so beautifully, "A lamp to my feet is your word, / a light to my path" (Ps 119:105).

Like the sacraments of Christ's church, the word contains a power that God has placed there. Its effects are not magical, but require an openness on our part to be changed. God offers us his healing and saving power through word and sacrament, and when the conditions are right within our hearts, we are gradually transformed. Jesus compared God's word to seed that is sown:

> On another occasion [Jesus] began to teach by the sea. A very large crowd gathered around him so that he got into a boat on the sea and sat down. And the whole crowd was beside the sea on land. And he taught them at length in parables, and in the course of his instruction he said to them, "Hear this! A sower went out to sow. And as he sowed, some seed fell on the path, and the birds came and ate it up.

> Other seed fell on rocky ground where it had little soil. It sprang up
> at once because the soil was not deep. And when the sun rose, it was
> scorched and it withered for lack of roots. Some seed fell among
> thorns, and the thorns grew up and choked it and it produced no
> grain. And some seed fell on rich soil and produced fruit. It came up
> and grew and yielded thirty, sixty, and a hundredfold." (Mark 4:1-8)

As Jesus explains his parable, we realize that there are many ways that
we prevent the seed of God's word from having its effect within us. But
when we prepare the soil of our hearts and create the conditions for the
growth and cultivation of the word, it will take root and yield abundant
fruit.

> The sower sows the word. These are the ones on the path where the
> word is sown. As soon as they hear, Satan comes at once and takes
> away the word sown in them. And these are the ones sown on rocky
> ground who, when they hear the word, receive it at once with joy.
> But they have no root; they last only for a time. Then when tribulation
> or persecution comes because of the word, they quickly fall away.
> Those sown among thorns are another sort. They are the people
> who hear the word, but worldly anxiety, the lure of riches, and the
> craving for other things intrude and choke the word, and it bears no
> fruit. But those sown on rich soil are the ones who hear the word and
> accept it and bear fruit thirty and sixty and a hundredfold." (Mark
> 4:14-20)

The word of God at work within us has an effect when we cultivate
it in our hearts and allow it to produce results within our lives. Paul
spoke about this word in his letter to the Thessalonians, distinguishing
it from a human word. With gratitude to his readers for their open hearts,
he tells them that "in receiving the word of God from hearing us, you
received not a human word but, as it truly is, the word of God, which is
now at work in you who believe" (1 Thess 2:13).

The word of God can work within us when we study Sacred Scripture.
The effects of the word within us are usually subtle but real. The more
we remove the obstacles in the way—our fears, impatience, temptations,
difficulties, misunderstandings—the more we will experience the transforming effects of the word. Usually we don't experience overwhelming
insights or spiritual ecstasies. More often we gradually become aware
that the fruit of studying the Bible is the fruit of the Spirit: "love, joy,
peace, patience, kindness, generosity, faithfulness, gentleness, self-
control" (Gal 5:22-23). When we begin to notice this fruit in the midst of

the way we live each day, we will know that the word of God is having an effect and transforming our hearts.

The Role of the Holy Spirit

Through the work of the Holy Spirit, the words of the Bible come alive when we read them. The Holy Spirit transforms those pages of paper and ink into the living word of God. The Holy Spirit is the link between the world of the Bible and our world. The Holy Spirit, who inspired the sacred writers of the Bible, now breathes within us as we read the Bible as the word of God.

The first disciples of Jesus realized that they did not have the capacity to understand everything that God had revealed to them. Through the work of the Holy Spirit, they experienced an ever-deepening clarification of the word they had come to know in Jesus. This is the work of the "Spirit of truth," of which Jesus said, "He will guide you to all truth" (John 16:13). As disciples of Jesus today, we are sustained by this promise and trust that God's Spirit will continue to guide us as we listen to his word with expectation and confidence.

In order for our reading of the Bible to be a true communication with our God, we should pray to this same Holy Spirit. Each day before reading the Bible, we can ask God's Spirit to breathe within us, to give us inspiration, and to guide us as we read. The Holy Spirit helps us read the Bible in several different but interrelated ways:

- *First, the Holy Spirit enables us to read the Bible as the word of God.* It is possible for a scholar to know all about the background and understand the meaning of a text perfectly, and yet not experience the text as God's word. Likewise we can learn lots about a text and think we can interpret its meaning, and still not experience the text as God's communication to us. Invoking the Holy Spirit enables us to read the Bible in a personal way, to understand it as a word to us, as a personal communication of God.

- *Second, the Holy Spirit guides us toward a true understanding of the inspired meaning of the Scriptures.* The Holy Spirit does not replace our own efforts, but rather guides our efforts to understand. The Holy Spirit begins by opening our minds, then gradually enables us to comprehend the meaning that God wants to communicate for our growth and life. When we are not sincerely open and docile to the movements of the Holy Spirit, we can easily begin to force our own private meanings on the Scriptures. But when we humbly open our lives to what God wants, the words of the Bible will guide us toward the understanding that God's wills for us.

- *Third, the Holy Spirit inspires our response to God's word.* The Holy Spirit works within us to allow what we read to have an effect on us and to gradually change us. Reading the Bible with the Spirit of God will not allow us to remain neutral. If God is truly communicating with us, then we must respond in some way. Sometimes it may be toward a deeper relationship with God in prayer. At other times, our response might be to change our actions in relationship to other people. Other passages might challenge us to act in an area of Christian life that we had neglected before.

Reading the Bible under the guiding light of the Holy Spirit makes our reflective reading central to our daily experience of following Christ. The words of the Bible can come alive as never before as God's Spirit enlightens our minds and inflames our hearts.

CHAPTER THREE

Choosing a Bible Today

There is a wide variety of Bibles on the market today. If we go into a bookstore, we see a large and confusing assortment of Bibles available on the shelves. Titles range from the traditional *Holy Bible* to the contemporary sounding *Good News Bible*. The binding varies from the leather-bound and gold-leafed to blue denim. Sometimes families have a large Bible in an honored place in their home, but others have several inexpensive Bibles that are treated no better than paperback novels.

This current state of Bible availability makes it very clear to us that God's holy word, the Sacred Scriptures, is not just a matter of the few thousand pages of paper on which it is written. God's word, rather, is a living reality, dependent on a personal encounter. Only when we respond in faith to the words of the biblical text, do we experience these many pages as the word of God for us.

This abundance of Bibles in different languages, versions, and translations has been very recent. Thanks to modern methods of printing and economical means of book production, the Bible can be easily owned by anyone. This has not always been the case. Through most of Christian history, Bibles were extremely rare and prohibitively costly. Few people could read or write, and few owned books. The Bible was experienced by ordinary people through the word proclaimed at liturgy, through preaching, music, and other oral media, through Christian art and stained glass, and other means that surrounded Christian people with the stories and traditions of their faith contained in the Bible.

Jesus, like the teachers and rabbis of his day, read in the synagogues from the Hebrew Scriptures, what Christians today call the Old Testament. Yet the work from which he read looked very different from the form in which we read the Scriptures today. Each writing was preserved on a long scroll made from papyrus. The Hebrew in which it was written would have looked strange to our eyes. The Hebrew language is written from right to left, and it contains no vowels.

When the gospels and letters of the New Testament were written, they too were written individually on long scrolls. They were written in Greek, with all capital letters, with the words run together without spacing or punctuation. Sentences were not punctuated until the sixth and seventh centuries, and it was not until the eleventh century that words were spaced apart and written separately.

We think of the Bible as a book. Yet, it did not begin as an organized and neatly bound book, but as a collection of separate scrolls. These scrolls were about a foot and a half wide and could extend to twelve feet or so in length. Copies of these scrolls were rare. Writing was done on papyrus, a paper-like substance made from attaching sheets of the reed plant together. Sheets of papyrus were costly, and enough to form a long scroll could cost several months' wages. Writing was very slow and laborious. A good scribe could write at a pace of about seventy-two words per hour. Paul's letter to the Romans would have required about a hundred hours just to copy!

The original manuscripts by the authors of the biblical books have long since perished. Like the other great literature of the ancient world, we have no originals, only copies. The oldest surviving edition of the complete Bible dates from the fourth century and is in the Vatican library today. However, thousands of older fragments and individual books exist, and many of them contain slight differences from one another. The work of deciding which reading is the most original is the work of textual scholars. Thus, making a modern translation of the Bible means not just translating an ancient text, but studying the many ancient texts and deciding which is the most accurate and original.

The Catholic and Protestant Versions

Nowhere in the Bible is it stated which books should make up the Bible. Certainly there have been many other sacred writings of Jews and Christians through the centuries than those contained in the Bible. The decision as to which books should be included in the Bible was made very gradually by the inspired community in which the biblical books were written—the church, guided by the Holy Spirit.

Unfortunately the question of which books should be included in the Bible still divides Catholics and Protestants today. Are there seventy-three books in the Bible, as in the Catholic version, or is the Protestant version correct with its sixty-six books? First of all, it should be noted that the differences occur only in the Old Testament. Both Catholics and Protestants today agree on the twenty-seven books of the New Testament. But in the Old Testament, the Catholic version of the Bible includes seven more books than the Protestant version. Those seven books are: Baruch, Judith, 1 and 2 Maccabees, Sirach, Tobit, and Wisdom. The Catholic version also includes expanded chapters in the books of Daniel and Esther. These books are called the "deuterocanonicals" by Catholics, whereas Protestants call these same writings "the apocrypha."

The explanation of how this difference came about is a matter of complex history. At the time of Jesus, the Jewish people used different collections of the Scriptures. The Sadducees accepted only the Torah (Genesis, Exodus, Leviticus, Numbers, Deuteronomy). The Pharisees in Palestine acknowledged a wider collection of Torah, prophets, and writings. The Jews living outside of Palestine accepted an even larger collection of sacred texts, written both in Hebrew and in Greek. These Greek-speaking Jews read from a Greek translation of Sacred Scripture called *the Septuagint*, since Greek was the common language throughout most of the known world at that time.

Though there was agreement on the core writings of the Jewish Scriptures, the Septuagint edition contained several books that the Hebrew collection did not contain. The many Jewish traditions did not attempt to fix the Scriptures into any clearly defined list until a century or two after Jesus. For this reason, the Christian church did not inherit any clearly defined set of Scriptures from the Jewish tradition.

The early church, as it began to spread across the world, generally read from the Septuagint, or Greek edition of the Scriptures. As Christian writers began to develop new writings in Greek, most of their quotations from the Jewish Scriptures came from the Septuagint version. Likewise, the wider collection of Jewish writings, especially the book of Sirach, was frequently read in Christian liturgy. Though there was discussion through the centuries of which books should be read as the Old Testament, the longer list of books contained in the Greek edition became the standard throughout most of the church's history. In fact, St. Jerome's translation of the Bible into Latin, which became the standard Christian Bible, contains this longer list of Old Testament books.

The question arose again in the sixteenth century during the Protestant Reformation. Martin Luther, in his translation of the Bible, grouped the deuterocanonical books at the end of the Old Testament. He said that these books are useful and good for reading, but not equal to the Sacred Scriptures. The Reformers mistakenly thought they were returning to the Old Testament used by the early Christians, since the Jews of Luther's time held for the shorter list of 39 Hebrew books. They presumed that the books honored as sacred by the Jews of their own day were the books that the Jews had always revered. Thus, the shorter list of books became the Old Testament of the Protestant tradition. A few years later at the Council of Trent in 1546, the Catholic teaching clearly reaffirmed the tradition that the longer list was the official canon for Catholics.

Though this was a serious point of dissention for several centuries, in our modern times it is not a major cause of division. Catholics understand that these books are not at the core of the Bible, and many Protestants have returned to the earlier practice of including the disputed books in a separate section of the Bible called the Apocrypha.

Deciding Which Bible to Use

How does one choose which of the many translations available today to use for Scripture study? There are at least thirty translations out today in the English language, and choosing from among them can seem an overwhelming task. There are two principal considerations when choosing a Bible. First, the Bible must be an accurate translation. It should faithfully give us the precise meaning of the original Hebrew and Greek texts. Second, the Bible must convey that meaning in English that is clear and readable.

A few decades ago, the choice between Bibles was very simple. Protestants would read the King James Bible and Catholics would read the Douay-Rheims Bible. They are both written in beautiful Elizabethan English and are classical parts of our tradition.

The Douay-Rheims Bible was produced by four Catholic scholars from Oxford who had been forced to seek refuge on the continent in the last decades of the sixteenth century. The existing Protestant translations in English at the time were unacceptable because of both their inadequate scholarship and their anti-Catholic notes. Work began on the New Testament while the English College was temporarily located in Rheims, and in 1582 it was published there. The Old Testament was delayed for lack of funds but was later published in 1610 after the college had returned to Douay. The Bible was translated primarily from the Latin Bible of St. Jerome. In general the Latin text was more reliable than the Greek texts that were circulating among scholars in those days. This Bible was revised several times and remained until the 1960s the standard Bible of English-speaking Catholics. Its last revision was published in 1941 as the Confraternity of Christian Doctrine Version. But soon afterward Catholic biblical scholarship began to blossom and translators began to work directly from current manuscripts in the original languages.

The King James Version was published in 1611. It was translated from the limited Hebrew and Greek texts that were available at the time. It contains many inaccuracies, yet it can be admired for the beauty of its English prose that influenced readers of the English language for centuries. It became the standard English Bible for Protestants of all denominations for over three centuries.

There are two main reasons why these older versions should not be the principal Bible that we use for our reading today. First, because these two Bibles were written several centuries ago, they are not written in contemporary English and thus are more difficult to read. The English language has changed in the past four centuries, and earlier English sometimes obscures the meaning for us today. The ancient prophets of old spoke in clear language, and the ancient writers wrote in the contemporary language of their times. Certainly Jesus and his apostles spoke to simple people in plain and understandable language, and the evangelists wrote the gospels in the common Greek of the time. Thus, we should read a Bible that conveys the directness that the Scriptures intend in the contemporary form of our own language.

Second, and even more importantly, these older translations are not as accurate in translating from the original texts in Hebrew and Greek as the more recent works. Scripture scholars have made significant advances in the past few decades in the study of ancient languages and the discovery of ancient biblical manuscripts. Modern translations are able to be much more accurate and faithful to what the biblical writers actually intended to communicate than was ever possible before.

Methods of Biblical Translation

There are two predominant ways to translate the Bible, and each of the many translations of the Bible can be categorized under one of these two. The first type of translation is called the *formal equivalence method*, or word-for-word translation. This type of translation aims at adhering as closely as possible to the form of the original writing. The translator tries to match word for word and phrase for phrase as closely as possible. This type of translation is found in the Revised Standard Version, the

New Revised Standard Version, the New American Bible, and the New International Version.

The other type of translation is called the *dynamic equivalence method*, or meaning-for-meaning translation. This type of translation is not so much concerned with matching words, but with matching the ideas and thoughts of the original text. The translator aims at identifying the meaning intended by the author and then expressing it as it would naturally be rendered in English. This type of translation is found in the Revised English Bible, the Good News Bible (also called Today's English Version), and the New Jerusalem Bible.

In general, the formal equivalence, or word-for-word translation, gives a better sense of the original text. Thus, this type of translation is better for serious study of the Bible. The dynamic equivalence, or meaning-for-meaning translation, reads more naturally in English. This type of translation might be better for more leisurely, reflective reading.

Formal Equivalence Translations in Modern English

- The Revised Standard Version, completed in 1952, is a revision of the King James Bible. It sought to preserve the literary style of the earlier translation, while taking account of the changes in the English language and the many advances in textual scholarship. It holds tremendous respect as a highly accurate translation from the original languages. There is a Catholic edition that includes the deuterocanonical books, and the translation is used in several study Bibles.

- The New Revised Standard Version, completed in 1989, is a new translation in line with the Revised Standard Version. The translators improved accuracy and clarity, and they updated the language to more current English usage. The guiding principle was: "As literal as possible, as free as necessary." They achieved a faithful and accurate translation that expresses the Bible in contemporary English. There is a Catholic edition and several study Bibles with commentary and extensive footnotes.

- The New American Bible, first published in 1970, has become the standard American Catholic edition of the Bible. It was commissioned by the American Catholic bishops and translated under the auspices of the Catholic Biblical Association. Both the Old and New Testaments have been revised in recent years. The translation strives for accuracy, and it is written in language suitable for both public worship and private reading. Its introductions and footnotes seek to reflect the most recent scholarship.

- The New International Version, published in 1978 and revised in 1983, is the work of evangelical Protestant scholars and is intended to appeal to a broad range of English-speaking people. The translators sought accuracy, clarity, and literary quality to produce a Bible suitable for personal reading and public worship and preaching. It does not include the deuterocanonical books.

Dynamic Equivalence Translations in Modern English

- The Jerusalem Bible was the first Catholic translation in English to be made directly from the biblical languages instead of from the Latin Bible. It was first published as a French translation in 1956 by the Dominican scholars at the Ecole Biblique in Jerusalem. Its excellent notes, cross-references, and introductions have made this a very popular Bible. The text itself was translated from the biblical languages using a meaning-for-meaning method, while the introductions and notes were translated from the French. The New Jerusalem Bible is a fresh translation with many improvements. The introductions and footnotes have been updated, and its poetic character lends itself to public reading and personal prayer.

- The Revised English Bible is a revision of the New English Bible. It was produced by Protestant scholars in Great Britain in an effort to create a Bible that is easier to read and that flows more naturally in contemporary English. As a dynamic equivalence translation, it is more concerned with preserving the meaning of the original languages than the word structure. The revision of 1989 is enjoyable to read and corrects a few inaccuracies and archaic choices of the first translation. An edition with the Apocrypha is published.

- The Good News Bible, also called Today's English Version, was a project of the American Bible Society. As a dynamic equivalence translation, it is designed to be readable and understandable. It accurately translates the meaning and message of the biblical authors, but it shows little concern with the structure of the original languages. It was written for English-speaking people everywhere, and its language is clear, simple, and lively. It is very readable, but is less suitable for serious study of the Bible. A Catholic edition has been published that includes the Deuterocanonicals/Apocrypha.

So Which Bible Should I Read?

Which Bible to read is one of the most commonly asked questions by those beginning to study the Bible seriously. The church has no official version of the Bible in English. The bishops encourage accurate translations and contemporary English, but we are free to choose from among the many good translations available today. The older translations, like the Douay-Rheims and the King James Bible, would not be good choices because of their inaccuracies and difficult language. But the others described above are all good and reliable translations. Each of them has their own positive characteristics.

Other types of Bibles that should be avoided are paraphrased and condensed Bibles. The most popular paraphrased Bible is The Living Bible. Its commercial success demands that it be mentioned here. It is the product of one man who did not translate from the original languages but simply paraphrased the King James Version in modern and readable English. Despite the fact that it is very easily read, it contains countless inaccuracies. He changes the text in places and even adds to the text ideas that are clearly not in the original. Despite its high sales and attractive format, the Living Bible should not be used as one's principal Bible, either for study or for personal reading. The same can be said for condensed Bibles, the most popular of which is the Reader's Digest Bible. One of its aims is to cut out all repetition in the Bible. Unfortunately, the result distorts the text because repetition is one of the most important aspects of biblical stories and poetry.

Another unfortunate fashion in Bible publication is the use of red letters for the words of Jesus. These so-called "red letter edition" Bibles tend to encourage the erroneous belief that the gospel writers recorded everything Jesus said like a faithful stenographer. In fact, these words are no more important or significant than the other words of the gospels that describe the works of Jesus. The whole text is inspired, not just the words attributed to Jesus.

One thing to always look for when purchasing a Bible is the full edition, rather than the reader's edition. This full version contains the footnotes and cross-references added to the translation by biblical scholars. We will see how these extra tools provide valuable help to reading and understanding the Bible.

The best choice for someone beginning to read the Bible seriously is a formal equivalence Bible. Because these are more literal in their translation, they retain many of the subtleties and nuances of the original languages. These shades of meaning become important when studying the Bible.

Yet, it is often helpful to have a second Bible. Comparing different translations of a biblical text brings out different nuances and gives us fresh insights into their meaning. A good second Bible would be a meaning-for-meaning translation. These Bibles are sometimes best for reflective and prayerful reading of the Bible, but they do not retain some of the complexities of the word-for-word translations. Both a formal equivalence translation and a dynamic equivalence translation are a good combination to have when reading and studying the Bible seriously.

CHAPTER FOUR

Exploring Your Bible

The word "Bible" itself comes to us from the ancient Greek language. *Ta Biblia* in Greek is a plural noun and means "the books" or "the scrolls." When the word entered the Latin language it became singular and meant "the book." Thus, the roots of the word tell us that the Bible is a collection of many books; but at the same time, it is such an important book that it needs no other name than "The Book."

The Christian Bible is divided into two main sections: the Old Testament and the New Testament. The word "testament" means covenant. The early writings of Christianity referred to the "old" or "first" covenant between God and his people Israel, and the "new" covenant in Jesus Christ. The Old Testament contains the writings that grew out of and expressed God's relationship with his people during the centuries before the coming of Jesus. The New Testament describes the new relationship that God began with all people through the life, death, and resurrection of Jesus and the establishment of the church through the Holy Spirit.

When we look at the division between the Old Testament and the New Testament, we see that the Old Testament is at least three times as long as the New Testament. The Old Testament is a collection of 46 separate writings that were written over a period of many centuries. The New Testament contains 27 writings that were written over the space of just a few decades.

The Order of the Biblical Books

When we look at the table of contents and see the list of 73 different writings in the Bible, we might assume that the books are listed in the order in which the events occurred or the order in which they were written. Since the first book, Genesis, deals with the beginnings of things and Revelation, the last book, seems to deal with the end of time, it would certainly be much simpler if all the books were arranged in such a regular and predictable order. However, the books are not arranged in that way at all.

The order in which the books were written, in fact, bears little resemblance to the order in which they appear in the Bible. Instead, the books are clustered together into categories and arranged very generally according to kinds of writing. For example, the books of the prophets are gathered together and then ordered according to their length. The wisdom writings are in another grouping, even though the individual books were written in different periods that span Israel's history.

In the New Testament, we might assume that the gospels were written first since they describe the life of Jesus, while the letters describe the church in its early days. However, many of the letters of Paul were written well before the gospels began to be written. Neither the gospels nor the letters are presented in the order in which they were written. The letters attributed to Paul are presented roughly in the order of their length, with the longest, Romans, appearing first.

The books of the Bible have been given their titles for a number of different reasons. Many of the Old Testament books are named for their subject matter. For example, Genesis means "the beginnings"; Exodus is about the exit from the slavery of Egypt; the books of Kings describe the history of the monarchy in Israel; Proverbs is a collection of wise sayings and good advice. Some books are named for their central characters, such as Joshua, Ruth, Samuel, and Ezra. Others are named after the author traditionally ascribed to them, such as Isaiah, Jeremiah, and Ezekiel.

In the New Testament, the largest collection of writings, the letters of Paul, bear the names of the community to which they were addressed. Paul's letter to the Romans was written to the Christians in Rome, Corinthians to the church in Corinth, and Galatians to the community in Galatia. Others letters are named for the individual to whom they were written: the letters to Philemon, Timothy, and Titus. Still other writings bear the names of those thought to be their writers: the letters of James, Peter, John, and Jude, as well as the gospels of Matthew, Mark, Luke, and John. Finally, the titles of two New Testament books describe their subject matter: the Acts of the Apostles and Revelation.

Special note should be made of those writings that include in their titles the words "first" and "second." First and Second Samuel, First and

Second Kings, and First and Second Chronicles were originally one writing, but were divided into two sections in order to more conveniently handle the scrolls on which they were written. We often divide large books into two or more volumes today for the same reason. In the New Testament these paired writings are separate letters written at different times by the same writer or to the same community. For example, the New Testament includes two letters written by Paul to the church in Corinth, two to the church in Thessalonica, and two to Timothy. Two different letters are ascribed to Peter, called First and Second Peter, and three to John, called First, Second, and Third John.

Understanding Biblical Citations

The way we refer to biblical passages today, by chapter and verse, did not come about until just a few hundred years ago. If we made a reference to "John 3:16" to an early Christian, or even to a Christian in the Middle Ages, we would get a blank stare.

The biblical books were originally written on scrolls with no divisions. Quotations from a work were identified simply by the name of the person associated with its authorship; for example, "As had been said through Isaiah the prophet." Or, even more often, passages were cited by simple phrases such as "Scripture has it," or "As it is written." For example, when Jesus quoted the words of God to Moses, he said, "Have you not read in the book of Moses, in the passage about the burning bush, how God told him, 'I am the God of Abraham, the God of Isaac, the God of Jacob'?" (Mark 12:26). Today we would simply cite that passage by saying "Exodus 3:6."

In earlier centuries, the church began to divide biblical texts into smaller units for reading in the liturgy. These readings would be introduced much as we do today: "A reading from the book of Exodus." But it was not until many centuries later that a standardized way of designating a specific portion of a text was developed.

Our present system of dividing the Bible into chapters was invented in the thirteenth century by the chancellor of the University of Paris, Stephen Langton. This system began to be used in many manuscripts of the entire Latin Bible and then was used by Jewish scholars in texts of the Hebrew Scriptures.

Once the system of chapters became widespread, it became possible to divide the chapters into smaller units in order to cite passages with greater exactness. The system of verses used today was first used by Jewish scholars in the Old Testament to designate small units of the text.

The division of the New Testament into verses was done by Robert Estienne in the sixteenth century and soon became the standard way of citing small units of the biblical text.

While this system of numbering chapters and verses is extremely helpful for locating passages, it is important to realize that it is not part of the original Bible and is not "sacred" as the text itself. Though the choices of where to divide the text is generally good, the break between chapters and verses is not always the best. In fact, occasionally a particular division of the text breaks it up badly. Many modern translations also print the text in paragraphs, often with headings and subheadings to separate sections or scenes that fit together. These additions are also helpful, but it is important to realize that these too are a modern invention and not part of the original biblical text.

Looking Up Bible Passages

There are a number of acceptable ways to cite biblical passages. The standard method of referring to a passage consists of the name of the biblical book, followed by its chapter number and its verse number. Thus, John 3:16 means The Gospel according to John, chapter three, verse sixteen. The most common form separates chapter and verse with a colon. Another alternative that is used occasionally separates the chapter number and the verse number with a comma or a period. So, John 3:16 can also be written as John 3,16 or John 3.16.

Most citations will use a short abbreviation for the book. This is not always as easy as it sounds. For example, Exod 3:4-6, 13-14 means "The Book of Exodus, chapter 3, verses 4 to 6 and verses 13 and 14." Matt 1:18–2:12 means "The Gospel According to Matthew, chapter 1, verse 18 through chapter 2, verse 12."

Helpful Additions to the Bible

If you have the study edition of a Bible, it most likely contains many helpful notes and explanations that will aid greatly in reading and studying the Bible. Let's look at some of these helpful additions to the Bible in order to become more familiar and comfortable with all that various editions of the Bible have to offer.

- *Table of Contents.* This page at the beginning of the Bible lists the seventy-three books in the order in which they appear. This contents page can help the new Bible reader find the various books of the Bible more easily. Sometimes this page will also list the common abbreviations of each book, and sometimes it will list the books in alphabetical order for the reader to find them more easily. A few Bibles have tabs that identify each book for easier location. Some people like to purchase stick-on tabs that identify each book in order to make their search easier. Eventually readers will want to familiarize themselves with each section of the Bible and where each book is located: which books belong with the prophetic books, which belong with the wisdom writings, where the letters of Paul are found, and so on.

• *Introductions.* Many study editions of the Bible have an introduction at the beginning of each book. These introductions are usually written in italics or smaller type before the beginning of the actual biblical text. Introductions give a general overview of the book so that the reader will know what to expect. They explain what type of writing it is, some background information about the book, perhaps something about its authorship and the time and place of its writing, and sometimes an outline of the major sections of the writing that will be helpful for better understanding.

• *Footnotes.* Probably the most helpful tool in reading the Bible is the footnotes. These are not essential for biblical reading and are certainly not part of the original writing, but they are included by the translators in order to help the reader and clarify some confusion. Footnotes are indicated in various ways, depending on the translation: by marking a verse with a small letter, a cross, or an asterisk, the reader is alerted to look at the bottom of the page to find a footnote referring to that verse or section. There are three types of footnotes:

1) The most common type of footnote offers a brief commentary on a passage or sheds some light on a passage that might be confusing. These notes are the results of biblical scholarship and can be very helpful to the reader trying to understand a difficult passage more clearly. Translations done by Catholic scholars will occasionally make a note to offer the traditional or doctrinal understanding of the church for a particular passage. It is very rare to find a passage where the church has given an official interpretation, but there are a few, and it is important for Catholics to understand these passages in that light.

2) Sometimes footnotes will offer another possible translation of a passage other than the one chosen in the text. Often a biblical text

in the original language will include a range of meanings that could be translated into English in a number of different ways. Obviously translators can choose only one way that they believe best expresses in English what the original author was trying to express, but they may offer another possibility in the form of a footnote. Sometimes the meaning is uncertain in the original language, and the translator has to make an educated guess from among several different theories, so the translator may choose to offer us another possibility in the footnote.

3) Occasionally a footnote will tell us that there are variations of the text among different ancient manuscripts. Because copies of the Bible were all produced by hand until recent centuries, there are often minor differences in the text when comparing one copy with another. In these cases the translators will judge which variation is most original, but will sometimes give us the reading of another ancient text in the form of a footnote to inform us of the other possibility. Usually such a footnote will begin with "other ancient authorities read . . ." or some other similar phrase. The few textual problems that remain in the Bible are often interesting, but they are never vital for our faith or central to Christian belief.

• *Cross-references.* Another important type of notation added to the Bible by the translators is called a cross-reference. These are citations referring to other places in the Bible associated with a particular passage or verse. Sometimes these cross-references are found toward the bottom of the pages like the footnotes; other editions place them in the margin next to the biblical text. There are two main types of cross-references:

1) Some references point to other places in the Bible where the same subject is discussed or that shed light on the subject at hand. For example, if some words or action of Jesus in the gospel can be more fully understood through a passage from the Old Testament, that passage will be cited as a cross-reference. For example, when Jesus is called "the Lamb of God," the Old Testament passages referring to the Passover lamb of sacrifice will be cited.

2) Other cross-references will refer to what are called parallel passages. The most frequent example of this type of reference is found within the gospels. When the same incident in the life of Jesus is recounted in other gospels, often the parallel account will be cited so that the passages may be compared. Other parallels are found,

for example, between the life of Paul as recounted in his letters and the parallel accounts in the Acts of the Apostles. In the Old Testament, frequently the same historical events will be recounted in different books. For example, the history of Israel recounted in 1 and 2 Samuel and in 1 and 2 Kings is told from a different point of view in 1 and 2 Chronicles. Such parallel passages are often interesting and enlightening to compare.

These are some of the types of help available to the reader when reading the text of the biblical writings. These aids vary with each translation of the Bible. This is another reason why it can be helpful to have two or more translations. You will be able not only to compare the text but also to compare footnotes, cross-references, and other supplementary material provided.

Take a moment now to look up Ex 3:4-6, 13-14 in your Bible. If you can't find the book of Exodus, look for it in the table of contents of your Bible. When you find these verses of chapter 3, check to see if your Bible offers any footnotes that will help you understand these verses better. Check also to see if your version of the Bible offers any cross-references for these verses, to compare these verses to other passages in the Bible that might shed light on them.

As you begin to use your Bible for study, feel free to write in it, underline, highlight, and make notes. A Bible that looks well-used and lived-in is a far greater honor of God's word than a nice Bible with gilt-edged pages that simply looks nice in the front room of your home. Bibles can be great for holding documents flat and pressing flowers, but God wants us to become familiar and comfortable with his word. The only way for that thick book to become the living word of God for us is to use it well.

CHAPTER FIVE

The Scriptures of God's People

Sometimes we are given the impression that the Bible descended from on high, given to us by God as the complete textbook on how to be the people of God. But this understanding prevents us from appreciating what the Bible truly is for us. God, in fact, was forming his people and guiding the history of Israel centuries before a word of the Old Testament was ever written. God did not reveal himself through a written book but through the lived experiences of a people. Likewise, God was revealed through the earthly life of Jesus and the formation of his church through the Holy Spirit decades before a word of the New Testament was ever written. The life of the church was flourishing through preaching, teaching, worship, and evangelization before written narratives were ever considered. God did not reveal his new covenant through a written book, but through the lived experiences of the church, the living Body of Christ.

The fact that the community of God's people preceded the writings of that community, in no way diminishes the importance or sacredness of the Bible. Rather, this realization helps us understand more fully the richness of the Bible and what it can be for us. The Scriptures are truly God's word; they express God's self-revelation and help us experience that truth and life more fully. But God was revealing his presence, speaking his word, and sharing divine life long before that word was ever given permanent expression in the Scriptures. The Bible was written and formed by the people of God: the Old Testament by the people of Israel, the New Testament by the community of Christ's church. The Bible did not form the community like a manual forms an organization, but rather the people of Israel and the community of the church formed the Scriptures through their experience of God in the events of their history.

The Bible was written of the people, by the people, and for the people. It is the book of the community of faith. The Bible is not just an objective book of information; it is the sacred literature of God's people, the lasting testimony to its experience of God. As a crystallization of the traditions of this community, the Bible belongs to the community from which it came. Therefore, to understand and experience the Bible in its fullness, we must be part of that community of faith. The church and the Bible can never be separated. We hear, experience, and live God's word in the midst of that Spirit-guided community that God formed through the living word. We safeguard the Scripture's sacredness when we read it and study it in union with the believing community from which the Bible came to us.

The Hebrew Scriptures Formed Over Centuries

The Old Testament was produced gradually through many centuries. Abraham and his descendants were a nomadic people who had no written documents to record and preserve their experiences. Moses, who led his people through the desert, and the tribes of Israel, who settled in the Promised Land, were a people who preserved their history in their collective memory. Through the songs they used in worship, the stories they told of their ancestors, and the spoken and memorized word, they passed on their tradition from generation to generation.

Only several centuries later, when the Hebrew people became a united kingdom did national writings begin to emerge. Like other nations they began to keep records, court documents, and histories of their military and international affairs. A colorful history of Israel's monarchy is found scattered through the books of Samuel and Kings. During the reigns of King David and King Solomon, authors began to develop the first written accounts of Israel's history from the beginnings. They looked back on the origins of humanity and the origins of their people with the eyes of their Hebrew faith. They wrote about creation, patriarchs, and exodus. These writings were told in several versions by different authors over the next several centuries. They were not gathered together into the form we know today until much later in history.

During the later period of the kingship, over a period from about the ninth century to the sixth century B.C., the prophets began to preach, calling Israel and its monarchy back to heartfelt worship of God, and justice for the oppressed of their land. These prophets had disciples who wrote down their prophetic words and established another type of writing that became part of Israel's literature.

The invasion of the Israelites by foreign armies gave new impetus to the process of writing in Israel. The conquest of the northern kingdom by Assyria introduced a deeper concentration of faith and worship in the city of Jerusalem. This greater unity gave rise to many of the historical collections found today in Deuteronomy, Joshua, Judges, Samuel, and Kings, with an emphasis on living out the covenant with God. The most important period of writing occurred with the invasion of the Babylonians and the deportation of God's people into exile in Babylon. During these years of exile, the scholars of Israel collected the old traditions and set down an ordered account of much of their history and worship. This period of great trial was also a time of literary creativity, and the core of what we know as the Old Testament emerged during these years.

After returning from exile, the priests of Israel edited this wide collection of writings preserved through the centuries and formed the Torah, the first five books of Scripture, as they have been handed down to us today. The next few centuries saw the continual writing of a diverse collection of literature called the wisdom writings. Thus, through a process of centuries, the community of God's people wrote and edited this collection of sacred writings known to the world today as the Bible of Judaism, the Old Testament of the Christian Bible.

This literature of ancient Israel is not just a collection of facts and details about their history. The writers saw far more importance in expressing the meaning of events than in simply recording information. To read the writings of the Old Testament is to be caught up in the experience of those events. We read these writings of the past so that we can become one with the people, experiences, and faith of God's people in the present. By hearing God's word through the Scriptures we can enter into and develop that relationship that God established centuries ago with his people.

The New Testament Formed Through the Life of the Church

The New Testament was produced through a gradual process, similar to that of the Old Testament. Its focus is the life, death, and resurrection of Jesus, in an effort to express what Jesus means for the world. Yet Jesus himself never even considered writing a book. The focus of his life was God's living word. He wanted his life and his words embodied in the lives of his followers. His personal revelation of God is the foundation of the community he formed.

Jesus promised that his Holy Spirit would be with his church, dwelling in it, inspiring it, guiding it. After his resurrection, Jesus commissioned his disciples to go out and make disciples of all the nations, baptizing them and teaching them. The Spirit of the risen Christ was sent first to inspire human lives, not printed words.

The early church was the community of people living out the word of Jesus Christ. They preached the message of Jesus, baptized converts, taught the way of life Jesus gave them, shared the Eucharist, held their possessions in common, and were guided by the abiding presence of Jesus through his Holy Spirit. For the early Christians, believing in Jesus and being the church were one and the same. Jesus had come to create not a holy book, but a holy people.

The mission of the apostles was the "handing on" to others of the message they had received. This handing on of the gospel message is the meaning of the word "tradition." This tradition is the very life of the church, the handing on of the living message of Jesus—his words, his deeds, his saving life, death, and resurrection. Paul wrote about his primary task as an apostle: "I handed on to you as of first importance what I also received" (1 Cor 15:3).

This handing on, or tradition, was done exclusively by word of mouth and the deeds of the church for a number of years. Jesus had taught through the spoken word, and his teaching and life were remembered, discussed, and pondered by the disciples after his departure from them. In the earliest decades of the church, accepting the gospel and becoming a Christian meant accepting the living tradition that was being handed on in the church.

Gradually this living tradition began to be expressed in writing. The earliest writing of the church developed through the liturgy. Christians developed songs and prayers that were used in their worship together as they celebrated the Eucharist. These elements of the common prayer of the church began to be written down so they could be shared among various communities. The letters of Paul contain excerpts from these early hymns, baptismal creeds, eucharistic words of Jesus, and communal prayers.

Very early in the life of the church, the sayings of Jesus began to be collected and written down. Selections from this written collection can be found particularly in the gospels of Matthew and Luke. Accounts of his passion also began to be written in order to memorialize his suffering

and death in the liturgy. Thus, the earliest Christian writings were frag-
mentary writings collected from the living tradition, the worship and
preaching of the early community of faith.

The first complete writings that came to be part of the New Testament
were the letters of Paul. He wrote these letters because of his wide travels
and the need to correspond with various communities, either after he had
parted from them or to announce his visit. The earliest of these letters
was probably his first letter to the Thessalonians. This was written about
A.D. 50, about twenty years after the earthly life of Jesus. During the
next two decades, Paul wrote many letters, exhorting, teaching, and
answering the questions of the many church communities that were
beginning throughout the known world. Many of these letters are preserved for us in the New Testament.

The first gospel was probably not written until after Paul's death.
Mark wrote his gospel between A.D. 65 and 70, in order to preserve an
account of Jesus' life in an age in which the church was being persecuted
and the original disciples of Jesus were being killed. During the next two
to three decades, other gospels of Jesus' life were written as the church
in different communities remembered and reflected on the words and
deeds of Jesus' life as they had received them. Each of the four gospel
accounts is unique because each is recounted by an evangelist addressing
different communities, in diverse situations, bringing different questions
and understandings to the life of Jesus.

John's gospel tells us: "Jesus did many other signs in the presence of
his disciples that are not written in this book" (John 20:30). The many
words and deeds of Jesus had to be selected and ordered by each writer
according to the distinctive contexts and challenges of each community.
A rich variety of writings expressed the diversity of the church in its
earliest development.

By understanding the gradual development of the New Testament
within the community of faith, we see that the Scriptures were not just
handed to us by Jesus to be the handbook for the establishment of the
church. Rather, the process occurred the other way around. The early
church wrote the New Testament, through the Spirit-inspired life given
to that community by Jesus.

The written word, then, became an essential part of the living tradition
of the church. Together with the good news preached, taught, lived, and
celebrated in liturgy, the writings began to be seen as sacred for the early
Christians, in the same way that they honored the books of the Jewish
Scriptures. Both the oral tradition and the written tradition came to be

seen jointly as what was handed down for the ongoing life and belief of the community of faith. Paul understood this dual aspect of the church's life as he wrote to the Thessalonians, "Stand firm and hold fast to the traditions that you were taught, either by an oral statement or by a letter of ours" (2 Thess 2:15). The life of the church is about handing on the experience of knowing Jesus Christ. We enter the mystery of his saving life for us through the Sacred Scriptures and through the life of his living body, the church.

The Stages of the Bible's Development

We have seen, through brief summaries, how the formation of both the Old and New Testaments was a gradual process within the community of faith. This process by which the books of the Bible were formed could be described as a series of stages: event, oral tradition, written tradition, edited tradition, and canonical tradition.

The Bible grew out of a series of **saving events** in human history. Some of these events are the following: the call of Abraham, the slavery in Egypt, settlement in the Promised Land, the monarchy of Israel, exile in Babylon, the teaching and deeds of Jesus, his crucifixion and resurrection, and the formation of the church. All of these events occurred within the context of a community of people influenced by the self-revelation of God and the movements of God's Spirit.

These saving events were handed on through **oral tradition**. The memory of the saving events was kept alive and venerated through narratives, poems, songs, and rituals passed down through generations by word of mouth. Each time an event is passed on through the spoken word, the speaker highlights its immediate relevance to the listeners by selecting, rearranging, simplifying, emphasizing, explaining, and dramatizing. You probably see this process in the stories passed on through the oral tradition of your family. Ancient cultures placed a high value on their remembered traditions and guarded them carefully.

When we realize that biblical events remained in the oral tradition for many generations, sometimes for centuries, before being written down, we may begin to worry about things like accuracy. We think that somehow oral tradition is like that party game where people whisper a message from one to another down the line until the message becomes quite distorted at the end. But this parlor game has no relationship to oral tradition; in fact, it serves as a useful contrast. What is passed down in oral tradition rests on the witness of a community. If the whisper game were played out loud, the message would not be lost because mistakes would be corrected as they were made. When a child in a Christian community prays, "Our Father, who art in heaven, Harold be thy name," we don't need to worry that generations after will mistake the Father's name for Harold. The community safeguards its oral traditions.

Eventually, parts of the oral tradition got written down. This **written tradition** is expressed in a countless variety of forms: stories, poems, songs, collections of sayings, ritualized accounts, and many more. This literature consists of written expression from many different people, communities, periods of time, and points of view. The ancient world did not place importance on the identity of individual authors as we do today. Most of the biblical writers remain anonymous. Authoritative figures like Moses, David, Solomon, and Isaiah became associated with Hebrew writings that continued to develop long after their deaths.

The **edited tradition** represents the stage in which elements of the oral tradition and the many scattered writings were collected, selected, and put into the form of a biblical book. This process of editing the results of previous traditions always involved including some things and omitting others. It entailed weaving together strains of different writings to create a coherent work. For example, the first two chapters of Genesis contain two different written traditions of creation. The second chapter, the colorful account of God forming Adam from the earth, followed by his creation of the plants and animals, is several centuries older than the first chapter, the orderly account of the world's creation in seven days. Rather than choosing one or the other creation account, the final edition of Genesis included them both, back-to-back.

The community's interest in the biblical content as it passed from event, to oral, written, and edited traditions was always to convey religious truth, the meaning and significance of events for successive generations. When the biblical authors were putting together the literature of God's people, they expressed God's action and human response. The past is remembered in order to help future generations remain faithful to the love God has shown in the saving events of history.

Some of the written and edited material generated within the community of faith became biblical books. This process whereby the community determined which books to include within its collection of sacred writings is called the **canonical tradition**. Gradually Judaism and the early church determined which books produced within their faith communities accurately reflected their religious experiences and beliefs.

To illustrate these stages of development for biblical books, let's look at the formation of the four gospels. The saving event was the life of

Jesus Christ. After his resurrection and ascension, the words and deeds of Jesus were expressed in a variety of oral forms, through the preaching, teaching, and liturgical life of his disciples. Gradually, these oral forms were written down to preserve the memories of the original disciples, to communicate stories and memories of Jesus from one community to another, and to proclaim the mystery of Christ at the church's Eucharist. Eventually, evangelists began to collect these writings in order to form complete and orderly accounts of the good news of Jesus Christ. Each gospel writer edited the materials available to him in a unique way in order to address the distinctive needs of his own community. So the four gospels each tell the story of Jesus from a different and unique perspective and offer us four different portraits of his saving life. As other gospels began to be written besides these four, the church had to determine which of the many gospels in the early centuries expressed its own faith. Early in the second century, the church shaped the canon and determined that Matthew, Mark, Luke, and John truly express the church's faith in the salvation offered by Christ.

Understanding these layers of tradition within the formation of the gospels helps explain the differences in each gospel and the type of truth communicated within them. It explains why it is misleading to think of the gospels simply as eyewitness recordings of the words and deeds of Jesus. Each gospel takes a different perspective in demonstrating the meaning of his saving life. Each narrates the events of his life differently, resulting in multiple versions of the same events. Because the gospels developed gradually in stages, from the historical life of Jesus to the four inspired accounts, there is no need to merge into one seamless story the birth, ministry, death, and resurrection of Jesus.

CHAPTER SIX

The Inspired Word of God's Church

We believe the Bible is divinely inspired writing. This inspiration of the Bible guarantees for us that God is present in his word and that God reveals himself to us through the Scriptures. It assures us that when we listen to the Scriptures, we are listening to God's truth about the ultimate realities of life and salvation.

"Inspired" literally means "breathed in" by God. It is the breath of God, or his Holy Spirit, acting through human authors, that makes their human words the word of God. Paul's second letter to Timothy declares what we believe about the Bible: "All Scripture is inspired by God and is useful for teaching, for refutation, for correction, and for training in righteousness, so that one who belongs to God may be competent, equipped for every good work" (2 Tim 3:16-17).

The teachings of the church help us to understand how God is the primary author of the Scriptures and how God used human authors to produce the writings God desired:

> The divinely revealed realities, which are contained and presented in the text of Sacred Scripture, have been written down under the inspiration of the Holy Spirit. For Holy Mother Church, relying on the faith of the apostolic age, accepts as sacred and canonical the books of the Old and the New Testaments, whole and entire, with all their parts, on the grounds that, written under the inspiration of the Holy Spirit (cf. John 20:31; 2 Tim 3:16; 2 Pet 1:19-21; 3:15-16), they have

God as their author and have been handed on as such to the Church herself. (*Dogmatic Constitution on Divine Revelation*, 11; can also be found in the *Catechism of the Catholic Church*, 105)

Inspiration means that God is the source of the truth contained in the Scriptures. Yet these human authors used their own talents in their own very personal and individual ways. The Holy Spirit worked through them to produce the inspired Scriptures. Thus the human authors also remain true authors and the inspiration of the Spirit does not affect their own individual style, understanding, limitations, or creativity. The church teaches both the divine and human aspects of the inspired word:

> To compose the sacred books, God chose certain men who, all the while he employed them in their task, made full use of their powers and faculties so that, though he acted in them and by them, it was as true authors that they consigned to writing whatever he wanted written, and no more. (*Dogmatic Constitution on Divine Revelation*, 11; can also be found in the *Catechism of the Catholic Church*, 106)

Human Limitations and God's Truth

While we acknowledge the beauty and power of much of the Bible, we must understand that inspiration does not mean that every part of the Bible is as "inspirational" as other parts. There are some parts of the Bible that are simply records and lists of information. It is difficult to be excited and encouraged by long genealogies and military reports. But just as some people are most energized by the stock market report in the daily newspaper, even the parts of the Bible that seem like dry information on the surface can be the entry into a deeper understanding of God's ways in the world.

Other parts of the Bible, instead of giving us guidance and comfort, can shock us. The violence, sex, vengeance, and retaliation that we find within the pages of the Bible can make us wonder how this can be from God. But we realize that the Bible is about the life of an ancient populace, and in the real life of every people there is war and battle, love and lust, tragedy and triumph. Yet through all that very human reality, we realize that God is at work. God's grace always outshines human sin. God works within human weakness, misunderstandings, and failings to gradually teach us the distinction between our inadequate human understanding and God's will for us.

We find within the Bible factual information that is not as accurate as modern sources of scientific or historical information can offer us. Methods of historical dating and technical descriptions in the Bible all reflect the ancient prescientific culture in which it was written. Some would want to label these minor inaccuracies as biblical errors. If, for example, the order of succession of Israel's kings in the ancient past differs in two separate biblical sources, from a historical point of view this expresses an inaccuracy. Often different sources of information were edited together, and occasionally these sources differed in their factual details. All of these are elements of the human composition of this literature. The writers and editors worked in a way that is characteristic of the literary methods of ancient cultures. Historical and scientific limitations and minor inaccuracies in the Bible should not be labeled as biblical errors; they are simply a dimension of the human aspect of the biblical writings.

The divine inspiration of the Bible does not guarantee the perfection of its human authors. However, because the Bible is inspired by God, we can have absolute confidence that the limitations of its human authors do not distort the truth that God teaches us through his word. While this truth comes to us through a human means that is less than perfect, the truth that God wishes to communicate through his word is "without error":

> Since, therefore, all that the inspired authors, or sacred writers, affirm should be regarded as affirmed by the Holy Spirit, we must acknowledge that the books of Scripture, firmly, faithfully, and without error, teach that truth which God, for the sake of our salvation, wished to see confided to the Sacred Scriptures (*Dogmatic Constitution on Divine Revelation*, 11; can also be found in the *Catechism of the Catholic Church*, 107)

So we see how profoundly the Bible is the product of both God and human persons. This means that the message of salvation comes to us through human history. It means that the truth of God is communicated through the unique literary styles of people. It means that the truth God wants revealed is without error, but that the manner whereby that truth is revealed is less than the perfection of God.

It might be much easier to believe that God simply dictated his word to human secretaries. But the process of inspiration is respectful of the ways God entered into the world through the humanity of Jesus. Inspiration means that God gave the human authors understanding, insight, wisdom, and the impulse to write, but left them free to think, to choose, to express ideas in their own unique way.

God guided the human authors when they wrote, but he guided them in a way that did not violate their freedom to write what they wanted to write. The guidance of the Holy Spirit did not prevent the writers from expressing their own individual personalities and viewpoints. Thus Paul, for example, can state his own opinion within his writings when trying to apply the message of the gospel to the practical problems and questions within individual communities. When he was offering advice about living the life of celibacy, he wrote: "I have no commandment from the Lord, but I give my opinion as one who by the Lord's mercy is trustworthy" (1 Cor 7:25). The biblical writers understood their own limitations and imperfections, yet God worked through them to offer us an inspired and sacred literature.

Inspiration should be understood, not just in relationship to individual authors, but within the context of God's guidance of his whole people, the church. The Holy Spirit guided not only the writers of the Bible but also the prophets, judges, and leaders of the Old Testament, and the apostles, prophets, evangelists, and teachers of the New Testament. If indeed the Bible is inspired by God, then the whole process whereby the Bible came into being must share in that inspiration. God guided the development of this whole body of literature that expresses the heritage of his people.

We cannot know the precise way that God inspired such a complex process of literary development. For many of the biblical books, God's guidance was present through many individuals spanning several centuries. If we try to read some of the Old Testament books as if they came from one author only, we will be faced with many difficulties. Changes in style, inconsistencies, and repetitions are all indications that these works are the product of a long process of development. When we realize that these writings are the religious literature of a people, we can appreciate the wonderful way in which the word of God is expressed in human words. As Scripture's primary author, God guided his people toward the final literary work that expresses his presence and truth.

The Bible is the Book of the Church

Some people claim that the Bible is the primary way that God speaks to people and, further, that the Bible is all that is needed for a life leading to salvation. This viewpoint, expressed by many Christians today, places the Bible apart from the church. It separates the Bible from that living tradition from which it arose. Some even say that the church is not necessary, or that the Bible is all that is needed to form a new church.

These views are certainly not supported by the Bible itself. The gospels clearly show us that what Jesus left behind is a group of followers who would be his living body in the world. The way to salvation, as the New Testament shows us, is found through becoming part of the apostolic church. This community of faith is how disciples come into contact with the living Christ present in the world today.

Through the ages, God has always been revealed in the midst of the living community that he formed. The word of God is handed on and preserved in the people of God. The word of God, the Bible, still finds its home today in the people of God, the church.

For this reason, the church and the Bible cannot be separated from one another. The Scriptures must be read as they were written, as the ongoing dialogue of God with his people. The words of the Bible cannot have their full meaning when read apart from the living community of faith. The fullness of the Scriptures is understood only by those joined to Christ through his living body.

We need the guidance of the church in order to read and understand the Scriptures. Interpretation of the Bible is not just a matter for each individual. Authentic interpretation takes place with the guidance of the Holy Spirit in the church. Through the church we are in contact with the message of salvation reaching back to the apostles. Through this living context of tradition, we can bring the message of Scripture to bear on new questions and new situations within the church and the world and within the circumstances of our individual lives.

There is an important distinction between "private interpretation" and "personal interpretation" of the Scriptures. As a member of the church, we are never really reading the Bible privately, even though we may be alone. We are continually nourished by the guidance of the church: its preaching, teaching, prayer, doctrine, scholarship, and history.

Private interpretation of Scripture disregards the context of the church, allowing us to understand the Bible in any way we choose. Private interpretation often leads a person to understand the Bible superficially, applying to the text any meaning that seems to sound right at the moment. The church rightly cautions us against such individualistic use of the Bible. All sorts of well-meaning Christians today are using private interpretation to make the biblical texts say many things that were far from the minds of the Bible's authors. This kind of interpretation can lead to much confusion, contradiction, and even abuse of the Bible.

On the other hand, the church highly encourages *personal* interpretation of the Scriptures. Through personal reading of the Scriptures, accompanied by prayer and reflection, we can begin to apply the message of the Scriptures to our own personal lives. After trying to understand what the Scriptures mean in themselves, as intended by the original author, we should always go on to ask ourselves, "What do they mean to me?" This is the kind of personal interpretation that will enrich not only our personal lives but our lives as members of the Body of Christ as well.

A Church Nourished by Sacred Scripture

Because the Bible is the book of the church, the words of the Scriptures have been at the heart of the Catholic Church through the ages. The proclamation of the Scriptures has always been an essential element of the Mass, and the actions and prayers of the eucharistic liturgy are rooted in the words of the Scriptures. The early church formed the New Testament and professed the whole Bible as its norm of faith. The earliest theology of the church, its creeds, doctrines, and writings, all flowed from the teachings of the Bible. The art, sculpture, and architecture of the church through the centuries have been formed from biblical texts. These visual arts were the Bible, in a very real sense, for the great masses of people who could not read, much less own a copy of the precious texts.

It is in the liturgy of the church, throughout the ages and today, that the Scriptures are experienced in their fullness. Great reverence should be shown for the word as it is processed and proclaimed in our worship. We believe that Christ is present in his word as it is proclaimed in worship. As the Second Vatican Council taught: "[Christ] is present in his word since it is he himself who speaks when the holy Scriptures are read in the Church" (*Constitution on the Sacred Liturgy*, 7; can also be found in the *Catechism of the Catholic Church*, 1088).

In its liturgical renewal the Council adopted a new cycle of Scripture readings for the Sunday and daily Masses. A three-year cycle of readings was adopted for the Sunday liturgy, during which a generous portion of the Old Testament, the New Testament letters, and the four Gospels is proclaimed. The same word is proclaimed throughout the world every Sunday, nourishing the preaching, prayer, reflection, and action of the whole church. Most of the mainline Protestant churches adopted this same cycle of Scripture readings.

The Scriptures form the norm for the life of the church. The church can test itself, challenge itself, and critique itself by the word of God. As the Council said: "All the preaching of the Church, as indeed the entire Christian religion, should be nourished and ruled by Sacred Scripture"

(*Dogmatic Constitution on Divine Revelation*, 21). Thus, the church tells us that access to Scriptures must be made available to all the followers of Christ, and the sacred texts should be the heart and foundation of the church's teaching, worship, and mission. Summarizing the role of Sacred Scripture in the life of the church, the Catechism of the Catholic Church emphatically teaches:

> "And such is the force and the power of the Word of God that it can serve the Church as her support and vigor and the children of the Church as strength for their faith, food for the soul, and a pure and lasting font of the spiritual life." Hence, "access to Sacred Scripture ought to be open wide to the Christian faithful." (*Catechism of the Catholic Church*, 131; citing *Dogmatic Constitution on Divine Revelation*, 21–22)

CHAPTER SEVEN

The Word of God in Human Words

John's gospel calls Jesus Christ "the Word of God." This means that God communicates himself to us in the fullest way through Jesus Christ. John begins his gospel by telling us that this Word of God, through whom the world was created and who sustains all things in being, became flesh and lived among us (John 1:14). Becoming flesh means that the Word took on the weaknesses, the temptations, the limitations, and the mortality that are the lot of humankind.

The church teaches us through the Scriptures and its doctrine that Jesus Christ is fully God and fully human. The Word-made-flesh is the very presence of God among us, yet he is human in every sense. If we claim that Jesus is not fully divine, truly we will not understand the significance of his life or who he is for us. But to reject the fullness of his humanity, even out of respect and reverence for Christ, is no less a mistake. He is indeed the divine Word, but he is the Word made flesh.

Likewise, the Bible is the word of God. Through the words of Scripture God communicates with his people in a preeminent way. Yet the Bible is also a human word. It was written by human beings in particular times and circumstances, with all the limitations and historical conditions that are characteristic of the literature of humanity.

The church teaches us this dual nature of the Scriptures:

> Indeed the words of God, expressed in the words of men, are in every way like human language, just as the Word of the eternal Father, when

he took on himself the flesh of human weakness, became like men. (*Dogmatic Constitution on Divine Revelation*, 13; can also be found in the *Catechism of the Catholic Church*, 101)

It might be much easier to believe in a word that miraculously descended from on high, rather than a word written by human beings over many centuries, just as it might be easier to believe in a God who descended to earth amidst dazzling wonders, rather than a God who came in the humility of poverty and suffering. When we listen to the word of God in Scripture, we must realize the full humanity of that word. Jesus is the Word made flesh; the Bible is the word of God in human words. If we undervalue either the full divinity of the Scriptures or the full humanity of the Scriptures, we will not understand the Bible correctly.

Literary Forms in the Bible

As the word of God in human words, the Bible is a library of books. Each of its books incorporates different forms of writing, different types of literature. Just as any library contains shelves of very different forms of writing—history, biography, fiction, poetry, essays—so too, the Bible is a collection of just such a wide diversity of literature.

The different forms of literature in the Bible express God's truth in a variety of individual and unique ways. For example, both the historical narratives of Jesus' life and the fictional parables in the gospels communicate important truths to us, but the truth God wants to express takes on a very different form in a parable than it does in a historical narrative. Both the fictional tale of Jonah and the writings of the historical prophets relate weighty truths, yet each expresses those truths of God in different ways. The same can be said for the poetic, symbolic accounts of creation in Genesis and the histories of the kings of Israel. God's truth is expressed in very different ways in each of these literary forms.

We easily and automatically make such distinctions when we read other forms of writing. We read an encyclopedia article very differently than we read love poetry. We read short stories differently than we read a list of instructions. Why is it so difficult to make such distinctions when we read the Bible? God did not intend the Bible to offer us a collection of factual knowledge from beginning to end. The Bible, rather, is a rich anthology of epic history, poetry, laws, parables, prayers, symbolic visions, songs, and proverbs. All of it is the inspired word of God. All of it communicates God's truth to us through the rich diversity that is so characteristic of our God.

Our church teaches us to consider the human dimensions of the Scriptures and to seek to discover what the human authors wanted to express in their writings:

> Seeing that, in Sacred Scripture, God speaks through men in human fashion, it follows that the interpreter of Sacred Scripture, if he is to ascertain what God has wished to communicate to us, should carefully search out the meaning which the sacred writers really had in mind, that meaning which God had thought well to manifest through the medium of their words. (*Dogmatic Constitution on Divine Revelation*, 12; can also be found in the *Catechism of the Catholic Church*, 109)

Reading the Bible as the word of God in human words requires discernment. We need to have some idea of the intention of the human author in writing a particular work and also the type of literature the author is using. We would make a serious mistake if we demanded that the parables of the Bible contain factual information, just as it would be a mistake to read the historical books of the Bible as if they were parables. We can be totally misled if we expect the poetic sections of Scripture to give us scientific information, just as we would be misled in reading the accounts of Israel's history as a fictional story.

Church teaching encourages a study of the literary genre of texts as an important means to determine the intention of the human authors:

> The fact is that truth is differently presented and expressed in various types of historical writing, in prophetic and poetical texts, and in other forms of literary expression. Hence the exegete must look for that meaning which the sacred writers, in given situations and granted the circumstances of their time and culture, intended to express and did in fact express, through the medium of a contemporary literary form. Rightly to understand what the sacred authors wanted to affirm in their work, due attention must be paid both to the customary and characteristic patterns of perception, speech and narrative which prevailed in their time, and to the conventions which people then observed in their dealings with one another. (*Dogmatic Constitution on Divine Revelation*, 12; can also be found in the *Catechism of the Catholic Church*, 110)

The inspired literary collection that we call the Bible has all the diversity we would expect of a religious culture that spanned nearly two thousand years, from the life of Abraham to the work of the apostolic church. Understanding the type of literature we are reading when we open any part of the Bible can carry us a long way in understanding the type of truth God inspired and the religious message God wants us to understand from the text.

Examples of Literary Forms in the Bible

- *History.* All forms of history are based on events that actually happened in the past. In this sense, most of the Bible is historical writing. Yet, we must be careful not to impose on the Bible the kinds of factual rigor that we place on historical writings today. The Bible is an account of historical events remembered and recounted in ways that were characteristic of the ancient world. Biblical literature contains a variety of different types of historical writings that express remembered events as part of a past held sacred by the people of God.

  The historical books detailing the *court history* of the kings of Israel and Judah are based on court records and oftentimes penetrating analysis. This court history is found in the books of Samuel, Kings, and Chronicles. These accounts are far from the detailed accounts written by today's historians based on the sources available from archives, but they are certainly accounts of real events, remembered and recorded by people concerned with preserving their historical traditions.

  Israel's founding story, the Exodus from Egypt, would best be described as *epic history.* This national story of Israel's liberation from slavery and formation as a people is recounted in every generation. Telling the story is a way to relive the founding event that made them a people with a mission. Epic literature, though based on historical events, typically focuses on the heroism and drama of the experience rather than the details of events. The highlights of the epic—the ten plagues, the crossing of the Sea, and God's revelation on the mountain—are told in ways that powerfully demonstrate that God was acting for the liberation of his people.

  The legendary stories of Israel's judges—like Gideon and Samson—are called *folk history.* This type of writing holds up the heroic and exemplary characteristics of figures from the past in order to teach virtues to the eager listeners. In the story of Samson, for instance, his strength lay in his total commitment to God. The outward sign of Samson's internal dedication is his uncut hair. Should he stray from his commitment to God, symbolized by the cutting of his hair, his strength would leave him. The lesson is not about appropriate hair length, but about commitment and fidelity to God.

- *Poetry.* Much of the Bible is poetry, which can be distinguished in biblical translations by its verse form. Poetry expresses experiences in language designed to evoke an emotional response in the reader. *Lyric poetry*, which expresses emotions in song, is found in writings like the Psalms and the Song of Songs. *Didactic poetry* is specifically designed to teach the wisdom discovered through life experiences. Examples of didactic poetry are found in Job, Proverbs, Sirach, and Wisdom. Some of the oldest writings of the Bible are *epic poetry*. The Song of Moses (Exod 15), for example, might be the Bible's oldest text, composed not too long after the experience of exodus. It proclaims God as a divine warrior coming to the rescue of his besieged people in a way that makes it memorable from generation to generation.

- *Prophecy.* Israel's prophetic literature originated with those called by God to speak a word of warning or hope in the historical context in which they lived. The pronouncements of the prophets were not meant to foretell some distant future, as is sometimes thought today. The written collections of their words consist of mostly poetic oracles condemning injustices and calling people to create a society of justice and fidelity to God's covenant. The truths taught by the prophetic writings are mostly ethical and can be carefully applied to people in every age.

- *Didactic Fiction.* The ancient world did not classify its literature into the rigid categories of fiction and non-fiction, as we do today. But what we would call fiction was certainly a part of the national literature of Israel. Fiction is characterized by the fact that it is drawn from the imagination of the author rather than from historical events. This "didactic" fiction is meant not simply to entertain but to teach important lessons. An example of this type of fiction is the story of Jonah. The wise and witty author told the colorful story of Jonah as a challenge to those who would try to place restrictions on the mercy of God or exclude other people from the scope of God's concern. Whereas the historical prophets condemned the prejudices of Israel with powerful oracles, the fictional writer of Jonah used humor and irony to accomplish the same goal.

    The book of Tobit is another example of didactic fiction that can be described as a *religious novel*. While the author uses a few historical details to provide the setting, the focus is on the development of the characters within an intricate plot. The families of Tobit and Sarah are Jews living in foreign lands who have been beset with misfortune.

The way the novelist cleverly weaves the stories of these two families together becomes a lesson on how God answers prayers in ways that we hardly expect.

The greatest teller of didactic fiction was Jesus. His *parables* are imaginative stories that came from his creative mind. But their purpose is to teach, namely, to get the hearers to change their way of thinking. Jesus told the parable of the Good Samaritan for many of the same reasons that the author of Jonah wrote that story. Looking at enemies in a surprisingly new way (the repentant Ninevites in Jonah and the generous Samaritan in Jesus' parable) challenges the hearers toward a new way of responding to them. Because we are not surprised by these fictional stories that we find in the gospels, neither should we be surprised to find works of didactic fiction scattered throughout the Bible.

• *Myth.* It is alarming for many to hear that parts of the Bible belong to the literary genre of myth. The problem arises because the word is taken in its secondary meaning as an unfounded or false notion. But myth, as a literary form, has an entirely different meaning. Myth is a traditional story that unfolds part of the worldview or ideals of a people. Far from being false, the myths of a culture embody its most essential truths. Myths deal with matters above and beyond ordinary life, concerning matters like origins, purpose, meaning, and aspirations.

Describing God's creation and humanity's sin in the opening chapters of Genesis as myth means that those stories express some of the most essential truths of the Bible. They are the foundational myths on which all the saving history of the Scriptures is built. Though Adam and Eve are representational figures rather than historical individuals, these accounts express profound religious insight about God's original desire for humanity and about human failure. Created from the clay but animated by God's breath, human beings are made to reflect God's image, to delight in God's presence, and to be stewards of God's creation. But humanity turned against God, bringing suffering, blame, guilt, and death. The myth teaches us that sin is essentially our failure to be who we were created to be. So, far from being false or untrue, the biblical myths of humanity's origins describe our purpose, our failure, and why we need salvation.

• *Gospel.* The word "gospel" means "good news." A gospel is a unique form of literature that is essentially a proclamation of the good news of Jesus Christ. The gospels are different from strict biographies of

Jesus, because the gospel writers wanted to tell us much more than what Jesus did from day to day. The evangelists were more concerned with expressing the meaning of his words and deeds than with recording his life with exact precision. It was only after the resurrection and the coming of the Holy Spirit that the historical life of Jesus could be fully understood. So the gospels are the written accounts of his historical life, told in light of the resurrection and under the guidance of the Spirit.

The four gospels tell the saving news of Jesus in four different ways, depending on the unique situation and concerns of the communities in which they were written. Each writer told the story with the intention of bringing the reader to an experience of Jesus Christ and the life he offers. The unique perspective and approaches of each gospel writer enriches our understanding of Jesus and his profound significance for the life of the world.

The Historical Reliability of the Bible

While we realize that not all parts of the Bible were written to record historical facts, we must not assume that the Bible is historically unreliable. In fact, the greatness of God's revelation to us is that it occurs through historical events. God reveals and discloses himself to humanity in history. The fact that the biblical writers were often more concerned with the meaning of events than with the details of events, must not lead us to question the historicity of every event. Unless God really did act historically to free the Israelites from slavery and form a covenant with them, the epic history of Israel could never have been written. Unless Jesus really did live and teach, and die on the cross and rise from the dead, the establishment of the early church and its writings would be useless.

One of the aspects of religious history that often concerns modern people is the rigid distinctions we try to make between natural and supernatural events. People in the ancient world did not make these distinctions about whether something happened through natural causes or whether God did it directly, what we call the proximate cause of events and the ultimate cause. Today, we would describe the cause of rain as clouds and rising warm air, but we also know that God is the cause of everything that creates the rain. When the plagues hit Egypt, allowing the Israelites to escape to their freedom, the Israelites did not worry about whether these were outbreaks that periodically brought affliction in the ancient world or whether they were a one-time-only act of God. The

Israelites never made these kinds of distinctions; they knew only that God was present, powerful, and loving. For Israel, all of life was an interaction with God, and God was acting in all the events of their lives as a people. The more we can understand that God is at work in all the events of our lives, not just the rare miracle, we will approach the understanding of biblical faith.

Suppose I saw an ant struggling mightily to carry a huge crumb from my picnic to its nest a long distance away. If I were to pick up the ant, crumb and all, and carry it to its nest within a few seconds, the ant would experience this as a supernatural event. What is supernatural to the ant is simply natural to me. Likewise, what is supernatural to me is simply natural to God. The distinction is simply in one's point of view. The ancients saw the hand of God acting in all the events of their history. The biblical texts that describe the intervention of God in the history of his people were natural events for a God who loved his people and wanted them to experience the fullness of life.

The whole Bible is about God's intervention in human history to reveal his saving love to humanity. Within this diverse literature is a variety of literary forms that express this great truth. For example, the book of Joshua says that the sun stood still (Josh 10:13) while the Israelites defeated the enemy. Understanding the literary form will clarify what the author meant. Because the image of the sun halting its daily course through the sky is a fragment of a poetic victory song, the reader will understand that this is an exclamation of God's power at work for his people, not a cosmological abnormality. Many past difficulties with the Bible have been rooted in the failure to recognize diverse literary forms and in the tendency to consider as historical fact pieces of the Bible that were never intended to be read that way.

Factual history is one type of writing; fiction is another. Both are found throughout the Bible as well as many literary types in between these two extremes. If we classify a certain part of the Bible as myth, legend, or parable, we are not destroying the historicity of that section, because it was never written as history. Neither are we weakening or challenging that section's inspiration. Pope Pius XII has it right in his 1943 teaching: "God can inspire any type of literature." Biblical fiction is just as inspired as biblical history because any type of literature can communicate God's truth.

CHAPTER EIGHT

The Challenge of Faithful Interpretation

The Bible has been called a bottomless well. We can always draw new refreshing waters every time we put our bucket into the well. Because the Bible is God's living word, no passage of Scripture can be exhausted by a single explanation. It offers fuller meaning and richness to each person and to each generation without sacrificing its essential truth. Studying the Bible is never complete; we always go deeper into its riches.

The critical challenge for all Christians is to learn how to interpret the Bible properly. The meaning of any given biblical passage is multilayered. But the primary layer of a passage's meaning is always that intended by the original human author in the context in which it was written. For this reason, interpreting passages within their original historical and literary contexts is essential for probing their meaning.

The Literal Sense and the Fuller Senses

The literal sense of a biblical passage is the meaning directly intended by the original human author. This literal meaning must be distinguished from reading the text "literalistically," that is, reading it on the surface without any historical understanding. Scholars probe the literal sense of a text by trying to understand its historical context and its literary type. This original meaning that the inspired writer intended is the text's foundational meaning. Any fuller or additional meaning discovered in a text must always rest on the foundation of the literal sense. There can be no shortcuts to understanding the inspired meaning of a biblical passage that bypass the human and historical aspects of its authorship.

In addition to the literal sense, biblical texts contain a fuller meaning that could not have been understood by their original authors. This is a characteristic of any classical work of literature being read at a later period and in a different context, but it is particularly true of the Bible. The people of God continued to see richer meanings in their foundational literature as they confronted new eras of history and new issues in their life as a community. When the writings were joined into the compilation called the Bible, this collection itself formed connections between the texts that no author could have foreseen, enlarging the meaning originally intended.

The understanding that God is the primary author of the Bible assures readers that the biblical texts are God's word for all times. This ongoing encounter over the centuries between the inspired Bible and the community of faith uncovers meanings in the texts beyond what the human authors could have envisioned in their limited circumstances and adds fuller meaning to the original sense of the sacred text.

The challenge of determining the fuller meaning of a text beyond the literal sense is the issue of authentic interpretation. How can it be determined whether a later interpretation is legitimate or not? When does an interpretation of the text cease to be exegesis (discovering meaning in the text itself) and become eisegesis (imposing a meaning on a text that cannot be found in the text itself)? The challenge of genuine and faithful interpretation of the Bible is an ongoing quest in biblical scholarship and in the life of the church.

The fuller senses of Scripture can never be derived from the text in a wholly subjective way. Any meaning that is alien to the literal meaning can never be considered an authentic meaning of the text. Fuller meaning must always be built on the original meaning and must be an organic development from the literal meaning.

Here are a number of different types of meaning within biblical texts that can be described as fuller senses:

- *The christological meaning.* The life, death, and resurrection of Jesus established a radically new historical context for all the texts of the ancient covenant. The new covenant in Christ shed fresh light on the Old Testament writings and brought them new meaning.

In the Christian tradition, this christological meaning has traditionally been called *the spiritual sense*—that is, the meaning expressed by the biblical texts when read, under the influence of the Holy Spirit, in the context of the paschal mystery of Christ. This distinction between the literal sense and the spiritual sense applies, of course, most often to texts of the Old Testament. When a New Testament text relates directly to Christ and to the new life that comes from his resurrection, its literal sense is already a christological or spiritual sense.

The christological meaning always demonstrates a profound conformity with the literal sense of the text, while, at the same time, gives the text a fuller sense. The new meaning does not replace the meaning of the Old Testament text but remains in continuity with it. Placed within the context of the summit of God's self-revelation, the ancient text retains its original meaning while expressing its inspired fullness.

- *The canonical meaning.* Although each biblical book has its own unique meaning, it takes on a fuller meaning when it becomes a part of the whole Bible. This fuller meaning of Old Testament texts was often expressed by the New Testament writers. Through quotations and references, they demonstrated how the ancient texts pointed to the new covenant. This canonical sense of the texts brings out the truth of St. Augustine's saying: "The New Testament lies hidden in the Old, and the Old becomes clear in the New."

  One way in which this canonical meaning is expressed is through *the typical sense.* This is the deeper meaning of persons, places, and events in the Bible when they are understood as foreshadowing future aspects of God's work of salvation. The "type" is a shadow or silhouette of the future reality. For example, the paschal lamb of Exodus is a type of the sacrifice of Christ (John 1:29); the passage of Israel through the sea is a type of Christian baptism (1 Cor 10:2). God's saving plan is characterized by a pattern of promise and fulfillment in which God's future realization is prepared through past revelation.

- *The ecclesial meaning.* The Bible developed within the living tradition of Israel and the church, and the faith of these communities found expression in its texts. God has used the Sacred Scriptures through the ages to shape the growth and development of the church. The ecclesial meaning of a biblical text is the fuller meaning of that text as it is understood as the means for continual growth of God's church and for its ongoing renewal.

When we look at the history of renewal within the church over two millennia, we realize that a return to the Scriptures has always been the catalyst and guide for the church's rejuvenation. The Holy Spirit guides the church to see the biblical texts as the incentive for new impulses and movements, bringing the church toward the fullness of its divine call.

Example of Multiple Senses

By examining the text of the manna in the wilderness (Exodus 16), we can see an example of the literal sense and the fuller senses of a biblical text. In its literal sense, the original meaning intended by the human author, the manna expresses the way God fed his people in the wilderness. The author wrote this passage not just to record a historical detail of the exodus but to demonstrate that God satisfies the hungers of Israel in every age. In countless situations where death seems certain, God is there with unexpected and wondrous food. This passage has a treasured place within the literature of Judaism, and as part of the Old Testament, it is also part of the salvation history shared by Christians.

As part of God's inspired word, the passage about the manna in the wilderness contains a fuller meaning than could have been understood by its ancient Hebrew author. In light of the mystery of Christ, the manna in the wilderness expresses a dimension of the salvation God offers in Jesus. Its christological meaning is expressed in the Gospel of John. Jesus proclaims, "I am the living bread that came down from heaven" (John 6:51). Jesus is God's gift for people's nourishment in a desolate world. While retaining the meaning of God's nourishment for Israel, the text also reveals the divine nourishment that God offers to hungry people everywhere.

Because this text is part of the whole Bible, we can see that the New Testament lies hidden in this Old Testament text. The text expresses its canonical sense not as a completely new meaning, but as a fuller meaning in continuity with God's work in the life of the covenant with Moses. Within the whole of inspired Scripture, the manna of the old covenant can be seen as a type or foreshadowing of the Eucharist of the new covenant, the living bread from heaven.

The ecclesial meaning of the narrative offers the church in every age the opportunity to understand what it is called to be. The manna in the wilderness challenges the church to transform the desperate world into a place of nourishment. As a eucharistic community, the church is called to be the bread of life that we eat, the living Body of Christ in the world, and to express the generosity of God for all who hunger.

Discovering rich layers of meaning in the biblical texts is part of what makes Scripture study so interesting and rewarding. The patristic writers of the church's early centuries, the first Christian interpreters of Scripture, considered their interpretation complete only when they had found a meaning pertinent and applicable to the situation of Christians in their own day. Faithful interpretation means seeking to understand the inspired Scriptures as the living word of God for our own day, but always in continuity with God's saving plan from age to age.

Considerations for Faithful Interpretation

Let's summarize some of the important considerations we've discussed so far for faithfully interpreting passages of the Bible. Good scholarship can help us with these understandings, but each person who sets out to study the Bible should keep these considerations in mind.

- *Interpret in light of the human author's purpose.* Since the meaning intended by the original author is the foundational meaning of the passage, we must always try to understand the passage first from the author's point of view.

  At the end of John's gospel, for example, the evangelist states his purpose for writing the gospel: "These have been written that you may come to believe that Jesus is the Messiah, the Son of God, and that through this belief you may have life in his name" (John 20:31). He wrote in order to bring us to faith in Jesus as the Messiah and Son of God, not to give us a detailed and precise biography of Jesus. By keeping John's purpose in mind, we will not be too concerned with why the order and details of John's gospel are so different than that of the other gospels.

  John's gospel, for instance, placed the scene of Jesus' cleansing of the Temple at the beginning of his public ministry rather than toward the end, as in the other gospels. In this way, the reader understands throughout the gospel that Jesus is the new temple of God's presence in the world. This same gospel places the death of Jesus on the day before Passover, rather than on the day of Passover, as in the other gospels. Less concerned with chronology, John wants to show us the relationship between the death of Jesus, the Lamb of God, and the sacrifice of the paschal lambs that were slaughtered in the Temple on the afternoon before the Passover began.

- *Interpret in light of the context.* We have seen how distorted interpretations can be forced on a biblical passage by lifting it out of its context. By reading a passage along with its surrounding verses and within the context of the entire book, we will be led to understand it better and not force a meaning opposed to the intention of its author.

  For example, many throughout history have taken Paul's words, "Slaves, be obedient to your masters with fear and trembling" (Eph 6:5), as biblical justification for slavery. But those words must be interpreted within the context of that passage, which is discussing how people in all relationships should be mutually submissive toward one another (Eph 5:21). When read in the context of Paul's writings, we understand that Paul could not be advocating the institution of slavery within the gospel of freedom that he preached so powerfully.

- *Interpret in light of the historical and cultural background.* An immense historical and cultural gap divides the world of the Bible and the world of the modern-day reader. Just as it would be very difficult for Jeremiah or Paul to enter the twenty-first century and understand our world, it is challenging to try to enter the world of the biblical authors. Yet learning something of the setting, situation, and customs of biblical times can help us immensely when interpreting the Scriptures.

  If we knew nothing about the Samaritans, we would read the parable of the Good Samaritan simply as a story about a good person who helps another person in need. It would be a good lesson, but not the radical teaching Jesus intended it to be. When we understand that the Samaritans were despised as foreigners and heretics by the Jewish people, the parable becomes a sweeping support for universal justice and love for the outcast.

- *Interpret in light of the literary type.* Like a library containing many different types of literature, we know that God's truth is communicated through a variety of different types of writing. In order to understand what the author is trying to express, we need to have some idea of the literary type he is using to express that truth.

  For instance, we cannot begin to interpret the book of Revelation unless we know that it is apocalyptic writing, a literary type that is written in situations of crisis. Knowing that this type of literature contains all sorts of secret and symbolic imagery, we can come to appreciate the way that God's truth is expressed in this apocalyptic style. Far from expressing a factual forecast of the future, Revelation presents a hopeful view of God's conquest in the midst of trials and persecution.

- *Interpret in light of the canon of Scripture.* The biblical texts take on fuller meaning when they are read in the context of the whole Bible. So, when we read a violent text of Scripture that doesn't sound like it should be coming from the merciful God we have come to know, we realize that every Scripture passage is only a small part of God's total word.

  When the people of Israel exact a destructive and vengeful conquest of their enemies in pursuit of what seems to be the direction of God, read that passage in the context of God's further revelation in the prophets. Reading about God's mercy and concern for all the world's people in the Hebrew prophets can help distinguish between Israel's historical context and God's timeless will for his people.

- *Interpret in light of the tradition of the church.* The same Holy Spirit, who inspired the original authors, continues to guide the church. As the community of faith in which the Scriptures were written, the church places us in the context of the ongoing interpretation of the Bible through the ages. We read in the light of the believing community, which has continued to understand new meaning within the text in every age. This tradition of the church is the ongoing life, teaching, prayer, worship, scholarship, experience, and reflection of the community. Without the community of faith, we could read the Bible only as another work of literature. As part of the community of faith we read the Bible as the revelation of God to us.

CHAPTER NINE

The Fallacy of Biblical Fundamentalism

Biblical fundamentalism arises when people disregard the historical context and cultural situation in which the Scriptures were written. People can make Scripture mean anything they want it to mean by cutting and pasting Scripture verses out of context and ignoring the basic meaning intended by their original human author. However exciting, interesting, or challenging such fanciful interpretations may be, if they are opposed to the meaning intended by the author, they cannot be valid. In fact, such simplistic interpretations of the Bible, as we hear so often today, are a serious abuse of God's word to us.

Refusing to take into account the historical character of the Bible's revelation, fundamentalism rejects critical research and scientific methods of biblical interpretation. By treating the biblical text as if it had been dictated word-for-word by God's Spirit, it refuses to admit that the inspired word of God has been expressed in human language by human authors possessing limited capacities and understanding. It fails to recognize that the inspired text has been formulated in language and expression conditioned by the time and culture in which it was written. In short, fundamentalism does not accept the human character of the divine word in human words.

It is important not to confuse biblical fundamentalism with evangelical Christianity. Evangelicals encompass a wide spectrum of approaches to the Bible. Certainly not all evangelicals are fundamentalists, and many evangelicals accept modern approaches to studying the Bible and accept the human qualities of the Scriptures. Generally, fundamentalism is characterized by a rigid, dogmatic, uncompromising, and often uneducated adherence to outdated perspectives in biblical interpretation. Yet, fundamentalism is difficult to define because there is no overarching authority that guides and governs fundamentalist communities and theology. It is highly individualistic in character and holds for only one authority—the Bible.

Characteristics of Biblical Fundamentalism

- *The Bible is the sole source and authority for God's revelation.* The fundamentalist holds that only the Bible can mediate God's truth and God's will for our lives. No other authority is necessary. The Bible contains all one needs to know; there is no need to supplement it with other doctrines, creeds, or moral teachings. The very notion of a historical and global church as the mediator of God's revelation and source of authoritative teaching appears contrary to the gospel of Jesus.

  This position that the Bible is the sole authority was a primary slogan of the Protestant Reformation of the sixteenth century: "sola scriptura." It became the primary characteristic of the Reformers' approach to Christian truth, in contrast to the Catholic assertion of the complementary importance of tradition and church teaching. Today, most Protestant churches, like the Catholic Church, recognize the necessity of tradition, human experience, and reasonable deliberation in understanding God's will and direction for our lives.

  The Catholic Church gives great honor to Sacred Scripture but does not teach that it is the singular source for mediating God's revelation. The New Testament itself was written in the context of the church and guided by the Holy Spirit. The fact that the church determined which books would be included in the Bible shows the necessity for an authoritative community to mediate God's truth and God's will from age to age.

- *The meaning and teaching of the Bible is self-evident.* The fundamentalist holds that any individual is capable of reading the Bible and receiving God's message accurately and fully. Because the Bible's plain sense is easily comprehensible, there is no need for outside assistance to explain what the Bible clearly teaches. The Bible means exactly what it says.

Of course, Catholic teaching holds for the necessity of reading the Bible within the context of the church's guidance. It warns against private interpretation, and makes available the church's scholarship and teaching as a help to interpreting the Bible. Since there is a clear gap in time, language, and culture between the world of the biblical authors and the world of today's reader, the meaning of the Bible is not entirely self-evident. While understanding the Bible is not an impossible goal, neither is it something that most readers can accomplish immediately. The church offers us the context of tradition, scholarship, and guidance, which makes interpreting the Bible properly a realistic goal.

- *Inspiration assures us that the Bible is written with infallible accuracy.* Most fundamentalists hold for the theory of "plenary verbal inspiration," the view that every word of the original manuscripts of the Bible is completely inspired and inerrant in every aspect. This understanding of inspiration is so absolute that the Bible could not possibly contain any factual, historical, scientific, or geographical inaccuracies or contradictions. Since God cannot err, the Bible cannot err. If the Bible were to err, even in the slightest matter, its truth would be totally compromised.

This absolute position, however, is asserted only for the autograph editions of biblical books, that is, the original texts. If it seems that there are textual errors, they must have crept in as an inattentive scribe was copying from an earlier text. The problem, though, is that the autographs no longer exist, so there is no way of knowing the original text with absolute certainty.

The result of this position is uncompromising on the plain sense of every biblical verse. Since the meaning is presumed clear and every word infallible, the popular bumper sticker makes sense for the fundamentalist: "God said it; I believe it; that settles it." There is not much need here for understanding biblical passages within their historical contexts. Since inspiration applies to every word, there is no possibility that it could have been said any better or any differently. The problems created with this rigid understanding are countless.

The Catholic understanding of inspiration respects the human and historical elements of the biblical writings. Certainly the Bible is inspired by God and God is its primary author, so that the books of the Bible faithfully teach the truth that God willed to express. We can be absolutely confident of that. But the human authors were people of their own time and culture, limited by the understanding of their times. Catholic interpretation is not bothered by incidental inconsistencies and inaccuracies characteristic of ancient literature. What inspiration guarantees for us is, not the historical and scientific perfection of every word, but the assurance of the truth that God wanted expressed for the sake of our salvation.

- *Only factual history is reliable truth.* For the fundamentalist, any challenge to the historical nature of biblical accounts is a challenge to its truthfulness. The fundamentalist often historicizes texts that were written in a form that never claimed to be historical.

  Because every word of the Bible is believed to come straight from God, every part is equally valid. To admit that any part might not be historically reliable is a challenge to the whole. So, for example, to question the historicity of the account of Adam, Eve, and the talking snake of the garden could be a threat to the historical nature of the Exodus or other historical episodes. To suggest that the talking donkey in the tale of Balaam in the book of Numbers might be legendary is as serious as questioning the historical reign of King David. To admit that any part is not historical is to question the authority of the Bible itself and thus threaten its sacred character.

  The Catholic understanding holds that the Bible is made up of a variety of literary forms. Each part of the Bible expresses God's truth in different ways. In fact, an important aspect of determining the truth that God wanted to express in a biblical passage is to determine its literary form and thus discern the intention of the original human author. God speaks divine truth through a variety of literary forms, some of which are intended to be historical and some are not. The mythological language of the creation accounts, the legendary literature of biblical stories, the symbolic visions of the prophets, and the historical accounts of Moses and David are all ways in which God communicates his truth to us through inspired literature.

- *Biblical prophecy is meant to speak about events for our day and prepare us for the end of time.* Because fundamentalists see much of the Bible as a matter of prophecy and fulfillment, they consider it essential to determine how prophecy is fulfilled through events in the world today. They are not so concerned with trying to understand what the passage might have meant at the time it was written.

  Fundamentalist literature tends to divide the world into good and evil, right and wrong. The forces of evil are increasing in strength, and worsening world events demonstrate that the climactic events foretold in prophecy will soon take place. The results of human history are preordained by God, and there is not much we can do about the impending cataclysm that will bring about the end of the world. True believers, however, will not be around to experience the terrible tribulations to come because they will be raptured to heaven to escape God's wrath.

This end of the world scenario mapped out by fundamentalists has no foundation in the Bible. It is based on a literalistic reading of selected verses cut from their context and pasted into a specific script describing current events. This apocalyptic script tends to focus on the countries and events of the Middle East, and its predetermined program does not allow for international diplomacy and gives little emphasis to working for justice. It is preoccupied with the Rapture, determining the identity of the anti-Christ, rebuilding the Temple in Jerusalem, and locating the site of Armageddon, rather than the imperatives of conversion, justice, and forgiveness.

According to Catholic theology, biblical prophecy is primarily addressed to believers alive at the time in which it was written. It is primarily a call to justice and repentance, a call to change and to seek God's will. As inspired literature, the prophets also proclaim important truths for every age, but their message is not intended to predict the details of a countdown to the end. God's will cannot be imprisoned in a predetermined script, and the time of creation's fulfillment is known only to God. The words of biblical prophecy and the teachings of Jesus about the end call us to always live in expectation, united in joyful hope for the coming of Christ and the completion of God's plan for the world's salvation. Catholic social teaching, rooted in biblical texts, urges us to be stewards of creation, to work for a just peace among nations, and to respect the life and rights of every person.

- *The Bible offers secure and certain answers in the midst of life's complexities.* Within the fundamentalist perspective, the Bible offers an emotional comfort to help people cope with the ambiguities and confusing choices offered by today's world. The Bible is a comprehensive answer book that contains all that is necessary for living the life that God wants. For a form of Christianity that is lacking in sacramental ritual, citing selectively-chosen Bible verses functions as a comforting practice that offers a form of concrete certainty. This assurance is reinforced in fundamentalism with the conviction that those who do not share this viewpoint are not really true Christians.

This simplistic approach to Christian faith contains serious weaknesses and dangers. In a document on the positive values of a variety of contemporary approaches to the Bible, the Pontifical Biblical Commission offered its only negative judgment to fundamentalism:

> The fundamentalist approach is dangerous, for it is attractive to people who look to the Bible for ready answers to the problems of life. It can deceive these people, offering them interpretations that are pious but illusory, instead of telling them that the Bible does not necessarily contain an immediate answer to each and every problem. Without saying as much in so many words, fundamentalism actually invites people to a kind of intellectual suicide. It injects into life a false certitude, for it unwittingly confuses the divine substance of the biblical message with what are in fact its human limitations. (*The Interpretation of the Bible in the Church,* 1993)

The Christian Challenge

The fundamentalist way of thinking about the Bible is winning more and more adherents throughout the world. People use the Bible to support their own social and political agenda in a rigid and uncompromising way. There are many ways that contemporary Christians can fall into the trap of fundamentalism. When we allow the words of the Bible to mean only what they seem to say on the surface, we are tending toward fundamentalism. When we read the Bible as if it had all been written in our contemporary culture to communicate to us enough facts to answer every question we might encounter in life, we are reading the Bible as a fundamentalist. Such distortion of the Scriptures must have been present in the early church as well. The Second Letter of Peter speaks about the writings of Paul when it says, "In them there are some things hard to understand that the ignorant and unstable distort to their own destruction, just as they do the other scriptures" (2 Pet 3:16). Simplistic Christianity has been around for a long time.

The Christian challenge is always to interpret Scripture faithfully, with the living community of faith guided by God's Spirit. The Bible is not a handbook of simple answers for life's complex questions. The Bible cannot be used as a weapon by taking passages out of context to defend one's own personal stances. The Bible must never be used to close minds; it must always open them.

A reverential approach to the Bible places us in the presence of the mystery of God. It calls us into the same relationship that God made with his people centuries ago. It calls us to experience the struggle of wrestling with God's word, allowing it to slowly change our hearts and transform our lives.

CHAPTER TEN

The Canon of the Bible

How did this sacred library of books come to be? We've already described some of the process that went into the writing of individual biblical books. Now we want to understand how these writings were put together to eventually create what we know as the Bible. Unlike modern books that are written in a short period of time, usually by one or more known authors, the Bible is the result of a gradual process lasting many centuries.

It was not at all clear to the people of God which of the many writings of the Israelite and Christian communities were to be accepted as the word of God. The books that eventually became part of the Bible had no particular glow that set them apart from the rest. Even the need for a distinctive collection of books was not at all evident to the Jewish and Christian communities for a long time.

The *canon* is the list of writings defined as inspired by God. It marks off the boundary between what is wholeheartedly accepted as sacred writings and what is not. The word canon comes from a word originally meaning "reed." The reed was used as a means of measuring and later came to mean a fixed rule or guide. So the biblical canon is the fixed collection of books that the people of God have determined to be its norm for faith.

The Spirit-led community of faith was the source for these writings as well as the authority that gradually came to see these writings as expressing its own faith. The inspired writings nourished the prayer life of the community, answered their heart-felt needs, and provided a rule of life. Slowly but steadily these books were judged as authentic reflections of the true faith inspired by God for the community. Eventually the reflection, inspiration, and authority of the church collected its literature and selected which writings were to be included in its sacred texts, the canon of the Bible.

Formation of the Old Testament Canon

The composition of the Old Testament was a progressive development that took over a thousand years. The earliest fragments of writing still present in our Bible, like the poetic Song of Miriam in Exodus 15, probably go back to about the twelfth century B.C. The latest writings, Second Maccabees and Wisdom, can be dated to about 100 B.C. During this long period of composition, there was a gradual accumulation of writings into books and then into collections of books.

The first complete collection of books to be accepted by the Israelites as the written word of God was the Torah. The written Torah, or Mosaic Law, is composed of the first five books of the Bible. The Torah was a collection of many strands of writings edited together to tell of Israel's origins. This first collection was complete by about 400 B.C.

The next completed collection was called the Former Prophets and the Latter Prophets in the Jewish tradition. The Former Prophets consists of the historical collection describing the conquest of the Promised Land and Israel's monarchy. The Old Testament indicates that there were other ancient writings that did not survive Israel's national disasters, and so did not become canonical writings.

The collection of the Latter Prophets, sometimes called the "writing prophets," is the written and edited remembrances of Israel's prophets. The entire collection of the Former and Latter Prophets was edited and collected together, and by 200 B.C. was accepted as part of the Jewish Scriptures. By this time, the two collections, the Torah and the Prophets, were customarily placed side by side, and the Hebrew Scriptures were spoken of as "the Law and the Prophets."

The most miscellaneous collection of literature is the anthology classified today as the wisdom writings. The dispute over which books should be included in the canon was most pronounced with these writings. By about 180 B.C., when the book of Sirach was written, it was customary to refer to the sacred writings of the Jews as "the Law, the Prophets, and the other books." The canonicity of some of these books was still disputed well into the period of early Christianity.

This three-fold division was ultimately accepted by Judaism. The Law, the Prophets, and the Writings are still the tripartite collection of the Hebrew Bible today. This Jewish Bible is called *Tanak*, an acronym for Torah (Teachings or Law), Nevi'im (Prophets), Ketuvim (Writings). In the first century A.D. Jewish believers read from these scrolls in synagogue worship on Sabbaths and feast days. A three-year cycle of readings, consisting of the Torah and the Prophets, with ample use of the Writings, especially the Psalms, was the liturgical norm for the Jews. The use of these books in Jewish worship was one of the major criteria for determining which books would be finally accepted into the canon.

Though there was a developing sense of canonicity within Judaism in the early periods of Christianity, there was no definitive canon of the Old Testament in these earliest centuries. The Christian church began to set forth the canon of the Old Testament in its early councils. In the fourth century, church councils defined the wider collection of writings found in Catholic Bibles today as the canon of the Scriptures. Yet it was not until the Council of Trent in the sixteenth century that the complete canon was solemnly verified.

The Collection of Old Testament Books

Let's take a closer look at this collection of books, which we call the Old Testament canon. Christian Bibles usually categorize these books under four headings: the Pentateuch, the historical books, the wisdom literature, and the prophets.

The Pentateuch is the first five books of the Bible, the Torah. It consists of Genesis, Exodus, Leviticus, Numbers, and Deuteronomy. The heart of these writings is Exodus, describing the formation of the Hebrews into a people through their exodus from slavery and through God's covenant with them. Genesis looks backward to the ancestors of Israel, to Abraham and Sarah and their descendants. As an introduction to the whole work, the editors poetically describe the beginnings of the world and humanity. Leviticus contains various laws, rituals, and customs used in Israel's worship. Numbers continues the wanderings of Israel in the desert to the promised land of Canaan. Deuteronomy is written as the final testament of Moses on the eve of his death, as the Israelites are about to cross over and enter the Promised Land.

The historical books begin with Joshua, describing the Israelites crossing the Jordan River and their conquest of the land. These books then describe the political history of Israel, beginning with the period of the judges. The period of Israel's kingship begins with the anointing of Saul and then King David. Following the reign of King Solomon and the building of the great temple in Jerusalem, the kingdom is divided, and the history of both Israel and Judah continues until their destruction. The later books describe the rebuilding of Judah after its exile as well as the struggle to maintain the ideals of Judaism in the midst of difficult times and persecution.

The wisdom books are a diverse collection of writings. Job is a magnificent work that confronts the mystery of human suffering. Psalms is a collection of 150 poetic songs written for prayer and worship. Proverbs is a collection of practical wisdom. Ecclesiastes is a rather pessimistic meditation on life and its purpose. The Song of Songs is a collection of love poetry. The book of Wisdom, the last book of the Old Testament to be written, was written in a time of persecution to inspire the Jews with the richness of their ancient faith. Sirach is a collection of moral instructions and wise maxims on a variety of topics.

The prophetic Books contain the collected oracles of the prophets of Israel. The prophets preached throughout the period of Israel's monarchy, speaking out against injustice and calling Israel back to the ideals of the covenant with God. The prophetic books are not included in the Bible in chronological order. The longer works are included first: the prophecies of Isaiah, Jeremiah, Ezekiel, and Daniel. Lamentations and Baruch are shorter writings associated with Jeremiah. The remaining twelve books are known as the Minor Prophets, not because they are less important, but because the collection of their work is smaller.

The Composition of New Testament Books

Today, Catholic, Orthodox, and Protestant Christians accept the same canon of twenty-seven New Testament books. Like the Old Testament canon, the end result was the product of a gradual and steady development within the community of the early church.

The heart of the New Testament, of course, is the person of Jesus Christ. He chose apostles to continue his ministry and proclaim his gospel to the world. These apostles became the living link between Jesus and generations of Christian believers. It was not until these apostles began to be separated from the living church, through both time and distance, that the need for writing developed within the church. With the acceptance of the Gentiles of all nations, the whole world became the field for Christian mission. Though the apostles traveled widely, this worldwide expansion created the need to spread the gospel message in writing as well as oral proclamation. As time went on, the apostles began to die, creating the need to preserve the memory of what the apostles taught. The early church realized that the written word was necessary to faithfully transmit what the apostles shared with their communities.

The letters of Paul are the first complete writings still preserved for us. Paul wrote most of his letters as encouragement and instruction to the particular Christian communities that he had evangelized. The earliest was his first letter to the Thessalonians, written about the year 50. Paul encouraged them to remain faithful and to correct some errors that had arisen within the community. His so-called Great Letters—Galatians, 1 and 2 Corinthians, and Romans—were written in the mid and late 50s. In these letters, Paul developed his understanding of the unique importance of Christ, the sufficiency of faith in him, and the new life lived in the Spirit. He addressed many different issues that concerned the early church communities: unity within the church, the eucharistic assembly, spiritual gifts, and the bodily resurrection. The Captivity Letters were written while Paul was in prison. These are Philippians, Colossians, Ephesians, and Philemon. In these letters Paul expresses his joys and fears, his convictions and anxieties, and urges the church to always live in a way worthy of the gospel of Christ. He expounds on the meaning of Christ in creation and redemption and on the unity of the church and its worldwide mission.

The remaining letters in the Pauline collection are called the Pastoral Letters. These letters were probably written in Paul's name by a later disciple of Paul. Timothy and Titus were co-workers of Paul whom he left in charge of the local churches. The three letters addressed to them speak about leadership, sound teaching, and pastoral care within the churches.

In his letter to the Colossians, Paul writes: "When this letter is read before you, have it read also in the church of the Laodiceans, and you yourselves read the one from Laodicea" (Col 4:16). Here we discover two important realities. First, we see that Paul recommends the exchange and circulation of his letters among the neighboring churches. We also realize that there were other letters written by Paul that have been lost to us. We know that Paul wrote a letter to the Laodiceans, and we also know from his letters to the Corinthians that he wrote at least two more to that community.

By the end of the first century, the letters of Paul had all been gathered together into a collection. The Second Letter of Peter indicates that his audience was familiar with the collected writings of Paul and that these writings were considered to be on the same level as "the other scriptures"

(2 Pet 3:15-16). Here we see that the letters of Paul were considered sacred and inspired like the Scriptures of the Old Testament, and therefore they were collected and read at the liturgy of the church.

The completed gospels came later than the writings of Paul. Yet it is reasonable to assume that much of the pre-gospel tradition began to be written down at an earlier date. Scholars speculate that a collection of the words of Jesus, sometimes called Q (from the German word, *quelle*, meaning "source"), was written down at an early date. Some earlier accounts of the passion of Jesus were also used by the church to liturgically remember the events of his suffering and death each year. The first completed gospel comes to us from Mark. It was written in the late 60s A.D., probably in Rome, and was greatly influenced by the memories of Peter.

Matthew and Luke both used the gospel of Mark as an important source for their own gospels. These gospels were both written in the 80s. Matthew's gospel, written for a Jewish Christian community, is particularly concerned with showing how Jesus fulfills the hopes and expectations of the Jewish people foretold in the Old Testament. Luke was written for an audience of Gentile Christians, addressing their concerns and describing Jesus as the Savior of all people. Luke also wrote the Acts of the Apostles, a history of the early church centering on its two main pillars, Peter and Paul. Acts narrates the church's beginnings in Jerusalem and its spread throughout the Roman Empire. The latest written gospel included in the New Testament canon was the work of John. He wrote in the 90s, taking a completely different approach than the other three gospels, emphasizing the divinity of Jesus and the importance of faith in him.

Why were all four gospels preserved by the church as inspired writings? Why not just choose the longest gospel, or why not combine them all into one? Each Gospel gives us a different portrait of Jesus. Each of them helps us to see different aspects of who Jesus is for us. Early attempts to harmonize the differences in these four gospels and condense them into one version were resisted by the church. The words and deeds of Jesus' life vary from one gospel to another, and the events of his life are written in a different order in each gospel. This fact demonstrates that the writers were primarily interested not in giving us a chronological biography of Jesus but, rather, in showing us who Jesus is and the meaning of his life. This explanation varied according to the questions and situations of the various audiences for which the gospels were written.

Finally, there is another assortment of writings in the New Testament, about which we know less than the gospels, Acts, and the Pauline writings. The first of these, the letter to the Hebrews, is of unknown origin.

It was written by a Jewish Christian to explain the relationship of the Old Testament institutions of temple, sacrifice, and priesthood, to the work of Christ. Then there is a collection of seven writings commonly called the Catholic Letters. These are classified together because they were not written to an individual community, but to the universal church. Most of these were written later in the first century and are attributed to Peter, James, Jude, and John. They deal with many differing aspects of Christian life: ethical conduct, the struggle to live Christianity in a hostile world, and faithfulness to the true teachings of Christ. The last book of the Bible, Revelation, is in a category by itself. It is written in a style called "apocalyptic," full of visions and symbolism. Its purpose is to give hope to Christians in a time of crisis and persecution.

Formation of the New Testament Canon

When and how was the New Testament canon determined? By the middle of the second century, the gospels and the writings of the apostles were being read in conjunction with the Old Testament in the Christian liturgy. By the beginning of the third century, the title "New Testament" was being used to refer to many of these Christian writings, and by that time most of the New Testament canon was recognized as inspired Scripture.

The earliest list of New Testament books that historians have discovered is called the Muratorian Canon, dated to about A.D. 180. In that list we find the following books: the gospels of Matthew, Mark, Luke, and John, the Acts of the Apostles, the thirteen letters attributed to Paul, the letter of Jude, the first and second letters of John, Revelation, Wisdom, and the Apocalypse of Peter. A similar list by Clement of Alexandria in about A.D. 190 adds Hebrews and the first letter of Peter. These writings confirm that by the end of the second century, most of the twenty-seven books of the New Testament canon had already been clearly established.

Yet, into the third century, there was still some flexibility in the New Testament canon. Disputes continued over some of the books—namely, Hebrews, James, 2 Peter, 2 and 3 John, and Revelation. Other books, which are not part of the canon, were considered sacred by some segments within the church—namely, 1 and 2 Clement, the Didache, Barnabas, the Apocalypse of Peter, and the Shepherd of Hermas. By the end of the fourth century, there was general agreement throughout the church on the present twenty-seven books of the New Testament.

With these many Christian writings, who determined which were to be considered uniquely inspired by God and part of the church's canon?

The same church from which the writings came also determined which of them would be considered its norm of faith. The process was gradual but steady, and over time the authoritative leadership of the church selected the twenty-seven books of the New Testament. This New Testament canon was settled using several criteria for determining whether a work is inspired or not:

- *Did the writing originate with the apostles?* Tracing the work back to the most ancient tradition of the apostles of Jesus was a very important consideration for determining inspiration. Today we realize that apostolic authorship is to be understood in the broad sense of authorship. It was not necessary that a work be hand-written by an apostle, but it necessarily had to be within the tradition of thought deriving from an apostle.

- *Did the writing express teachings for the whole church?* Writings that were significant only for a particular community were not preserved as carefully, while those that contained a message that applied to all the churches were circulated and became widely known.

- *Was the writing used for liturgical reading?* Those works that were read regularly as the church gathered for Eucharist came to be seen as sacred. Soon these writings came to enjoy the same sacred status as the inspired writings of the Jewish Scriptures that had always been read in the synagogue and at the worship of Jewish Christians.

- *Did the writing faithfully reflect the Church's life of faith?* Some works were rejected from the canon because they were doctrinally questionable or contained esoteric messages. Those works that expressed the tradition that had been handed down through the church from the apostles were understood to be inspired writings. The church saw its own truth reflected in these writings.

In this way, the church determined its own sacred writings. The community, led by its bishops scattered throughout the Roman world, came to realize that these writings were inspired by God and proclaimed the truth that God wished to reveal to the world through Jesus Christ. The church cherished this canon of sacred writings as its standard for discerning God's continuing presence and revelation within the community of faith. The Bible, with its canon settled by the same apostolic community who wrote it, became the anchor of the church's living tradition.

CHAPTER ELEVEN

The Importance of Biblical Scholarship

In a scene from the Acts of the Apostles, Philip encountered an Ethiopian official reading from the scroll of Isaiah. Philip asked him, "Do you understand what you are reading?" The official replied, "How can I, unless someone instructs me?" (Acts 8:27-31). Those who want to study the Bible seek that same guidance. But with all the words being spoken and the books being written about the Bible today, who can instruct us on what it really means?

Studying the Bible within the context of the church means reading it with the assistance of the church's guidance. Part of that guidance is found in the community of biblical scholars who dedicate their lives to helping us understand the Bible. This tradition of scholarship, guided by the teachings of the church, does the work that Philip did for the Ethiopian. Biblical scholars instruct us about the meaning of the biblical texts so that we may come to understand them.

In our day, many methods of scholarship have become available to us that can help us, better than ever before. In 1943, Pope Pius XII wrote an encyclical entitled *Divino Afflante Spiritu*. This broke new ground by encouraging new methods of biblical scholarship within the Catholic Church. He approved new scientific research, literary criticism, and historical study to shed new light on the meaning of the biblical texts. In that teaching, Pope Pius XII wrote:

> Let the interpreter, with all care and without neglecting any light
> derived from recent research, endeavor to determine the peculiar
> character and circumstances of the sacred writer, the age in which he
> lived, the sources written and oral to which he had recourse, and the
> forms of expression he employed.

This teaching was reinforced and expanded by the Second Vatican
Council and in the church's teaching into our present century. The church
urges us to make use of the many methods available today to interpret
and understand the Sacred Scriptures. The Bible is a vast treasure that
opens itself in new ways in every age. The biblical scholarship that is
available within the church today is an important means to study the
Bible with integrity and fidelity to the meaning that it continually reveals
to us.

Author, Text, and Audience

The communication of God's word has three principal components:
the author, the text, and the audience. In the biblical period, when the
author came from the same community as the audience, there was little
need for interpretation of the text. But with the separation of the biblical
text from the community in which it was written, extensive efforts at
interpretation have become necessary. The work of interpreting the Bible
today is largely a matter of bridging the gap between the world of the
author and the world of the modern audience, the reader of the Bible
today.

This divorce of the text from the original author and the original audience allowed the text to take on a life of its own. As a result, the biblical
message has been interpreted in many different ways throughout history. Many of these interpretations go beyond what the author originally
intended, as the reader finds a depth of meaning in the text that could
not have been understood in the historical situation in which it was
written. This indicates that sacred texts have a fuller meaning that could
not have been known by the original author. The constant challenge is
to interpret the text in a way that is faithful to both its human and divine
character.

Even throughout the biblical period, older texts were continually re-
interpreted to apply to new situations. The Exodus event, for instance,
was interpreted in light of new events throughout the history of Israel.
The Exile in Babylon, centuries after the Exodus, was understood by
reading the Exodus tradition in a new way within a new context. The

death of Jesus was understood by interpreting the Passover and sacrifice traditions of Israel in new ways. Since God is the primary author of Scripture, God can speak to the present through the scriptural record of the past. This has always led to the interpretation of passages in a fuller sense than what the human author intended at the time it was written. Because the Bible is the word of God, it has a richness of meaning that can be discovered in every age.

When the Bible was interpreted by the first theologians, the church fathers of the first few centuries, they considered their work satisfactory only when they had found a meaning in the text relevant to the situation of Christians in their own day. Scholarship is faithful to the purpose of biblical texts, not only when it goes to the heart of the Scripture to find biblical truth expressed there, but also when it links this truth to the experience of faith in the world today.

Some scholars maintain that the "real" meaning of a text is the meaning intended by the original author—what the text *meant*. Others maintain that the real meaning is found in the text as it is understood by the audience—what the text *means*. Most contemporary Catholic scholarship tries to include both of these poles in interpretation.

There is the danger of abuse, however, in trying to understand the meaning of a text solely in the context of the contemporary world. People misuse the Bible when they force meanings on it in line with their own agenda. Reading into a text something that is not there is called "eisegesis," whereas "exegesis," genuine interpretation, means drawing out what is present in the text itself. The Bible can be made to mean anything someone wants it to mean when interpreted outside the guidelines established by church teaching and solid scholarship. A superficial reading of the text can lead to countless false and mistaken interpretations. The difference between the world of the author and the world of the reader must be respected, and interpreters must utilize the many means available to understand the ancient time, language, and culture.

Fortunately, the Catholic Church has a set of official teachings about the Bible that clearly lay out the parameters of biblical interpretation. In addition, the church has an authorized agency called the Pontifical Biblical Commission, charged with oversight in the area of biblical studies and interpretation. This commission, founded in 1902 by Pope Leo XIII, consists of an international team of biblical scholars who guide and encourage biblical studies in line with the authoritative teachings of the church.

Discovering What the Text Meant—
The Historical-Critical Approach

The Catholic Church maintains that interpretation of a passage must be based on the meaning intended by its original author. This method fully respects the human aspects of the Scriptures by giving attention to the historical development of biblical texts across the passage of time. Basing biblical interpretation on its original meaning at the time it was written prevents interpretations that are too imaginative or individualistic. This does not imply that the full meaning of a text is limited to its historical meaning; rather, its full meaning must always be grounded in the message the authors addressed to their first readers.

The historical-critical method is a process of biblical study that attempts to get back to the world of the original author so that we can better understand the meaning of the text as that author intended. This method sheds light on the historical process that resulted in the final form of the biblical text. It attempts to bridge the immense historical and cultural gap between the biblical authors and modern readers.

Please note that when the word "critical" is used in reference to biblical scholarship, it is not intended to be understood in a negative sense. It simply means "intellectually careful." The word "criticism" here does not mean negative judgment or finding fault. Rather, it means "careful judgment and thoughtful evaluation."

- *Textual criticism.* Since no manuscripts that we have today contain the original texts of the Bible, scholars analyze all the copies available in order to reconstruct the original wording of the biblical text. This requires painstaking comparison of ancient manuscripts that have transmitted the biblical texts down through the ages. This is the first task of scholarship, since before any interpretation of the text can be made, the most accurate text possible must be established.

- *Form criticism.* This type of study tries to reconstruct the oral tradition behind the written text. It wants to shed light on how the biblical materials were remembered and how they were used before they were put into writing. Its first task is to isolate the individual units that make up the biblical text. These units are then classified according to their literary type, which helps to understand the context or situation in which they were used. Many texts, for example, have their original setting in the worship of the community, the temple of ancient Israel or the eucharistic liturgies of the church. Other texts, like the creation accounts, derive their forms from the myths of other cultures. These original forms were given new shape and new content in order to express certain truths of faith.

• *Source criticism.* This process seeks to discover the origins of the materials used by the biblical authors in their writings. For example, many scholars point to evidence that the first five books of the Bible are made up of several major sources that were woven together in the final composition of the books. The fact that these books were edited from various sources, rather than composed by one author, explains why there are differences in vocabulary and style within each book, and why a story often is told twice in different ways. For example, the first two chapters of Genesis seem to contain two accounts of creation because the editor combined a more recent source in the first chapter with an older source in the second.

• *Redaction criticism.* This process analyzes how written sources were edited together to form the final work. The editors, or redactors, gathered, selected, and wove different writings together to form the biblical book. From studying the gospels of Matthew, Mark, and Luke, for example, scholars have determined that Mark was written first and that Matthew and Luke used Mark as their primary source. Redaction criticism studies how Matthew and Luke used their sources, selected their material, and composed unique gospels with different purposes and emphases than the others.

• *Historical criticism.* In this method, scholars study the biblical texts to determine their value as historical accounts. It seeks to reconstruct the historical situation of the writer and the community of the time. It uses dating techniques, archeology, and geography. Biblical archeology is a fairly new science begun in the nineteenth century. By excavating the actual sites of biblical events, archeology can tell us more about the situation at the time of events. Often archeology serves to verify information we receive from the Bible; often it adds to our information and makes the background to the Bible more complete.

The historical-critical method of scholarship has helped us better understand the life and beliefs of ancient Israel and early Christianity. It has brought the people of those times into sharper focus and helped us understand the world out of which the biblical literature was written.

This method has enabled us to know more precisely what the Bible meant when it came from the creative minds of its original human authors and editors, and thus helped us to understand the truth of Scripture more precisely.

Discovering What the Text Means— Other Methods of Scholarship

The historical-critical method studies the historical process that led to the text as we have it in the Bible by trying to go back to the world from which the text came. Yet, we know that the meaning of a text is not limited by what it meant at the time it was written. Other methods of scholarship study the message contained in the text independent of its historical origin. Rather than tell us what the text *meant*, these methods help us understand what the text *means*.

No method of biblical study is fully adequate to comprehend the biblical texts in all their richness. For that reason, a plurality of old and new methods of study are used in biblical scholarship today. We need methods to show us the historical origins of the texts as well as methods that study the text in their final form, because this finished stage of development is the expression of the word of God to us.

Here are a few methods that study the biblical text in its final form in order to understand what it means for the reader of every age:

- *Literary criticism.* What is important in these literary methods is how the readers understand the Bible in their own times. The scholar is interested in how a reader responds to a given text, what effect the text has on the person, and how the meaning of a text emerges out of the engagement of the reader with the text. Narrative analysis, rhetorical analysis, and reader-response analysis correspond to these interests. These new forms of literary criticism show us how a work of literature has its own meaning once it leaves the hands of its author. By studying the text itself, independent of its historical background, scholars show how the work of literature itself can have further meaning as it is received by the reader.

- *Canonical criticism.* This study is concerned with the fuller meaning of a biblical text when it is joined to the other books in the canon of Scripture. It looks at how the text's final form was created within the believing community of Judaism or Christianity and how the meanings created by that final form continue to guide the understanding of that community. It interprets each text in light of the whole Bible, and so reads the texts in relationship to the single plan of God made known in the Scriptures as a whole.

In reading the book of Isaiah, for example, historical criticism tries to distinguish which parts come from the eighth-century prophet, the sixth-century prophet, and the fifth-century prophet. Literary and canonical critics, on the other hand, focus on how the final form of the book demonstrates a movement from judgment to salvation and prepares for God's universal salvation in Christ.

- *Feminist and liberationist criticism.* Readers always pay attention to those texts that speak to their own concerns and, without being aware of it, neglect others. Today, women are discovering new meaning in biblical texts unknown in a previously masculine-dominated scholarship and ministry. Feminist scholars today critique parts of the Bible that seem to undermine the full value of women and distinguish them from the liberating values of the Bible's primary message. They also highlight texts that speak to the concerns of women that were previously neglected.

  Likewise, those who read the Scriptures in developing areas of the world find new meaning that had been neglected in the context of more affluent cultures. People in a situation of political, economic, or religious oppression read the Bible quite differently than those from a secure and comfortable vantage point. The lowly ones of the world, who might trust in God more concretely, have a capacity for hearing the word of God in a way that enriches the whole church. The inspired text nourishes all God's people in the midst of their struggles and hopes.

- *Study of the text through cultural anthropology.* This type of study looks at the social contexts of human life in areas like worship, art, celebration, feasts, domestic life, commerce, rites of passage, taboos, sources of power, and human relationships, like owner-slave, husband-wife, patron-client, and landlord-tenant. Applied to biblical study, this allows scholars to distinguish more clearly elements of biblical truth that are permanent from those that are features of certain cultures.

- *Study of the history of the text's influence.* This approach is interested in the influence of the biblical text on readers in different periods and contexts. Whereas a historical-critical scholar is interested in the history of a text's development until its final form, this study is looking at the history of a text that begins after it leaves the hands of its author. The reader of a biblical text always belongs to a particular tradition, which provides questions and concerns that give life and meaning to the text. For example, we could study how Exodus has been read by medieval Jews, by American slaves, by Latin American revolutionaries, and by Zionists. This study also illustrates how false and biased interpretations have become prevalent—for example, those that promoted anti-Semitism, racial discrimination, the devaluing of women, or end-of-the-world delusions.

Whether discerning what the text meant or what it means, the constant factor in all the meaning discovered in Scripture is the community of faith. It is the community of faith from which the text was formed, it is the community of faith that accepted the text into its Sacred Scriptures, and it is the community of faith that continues to receive the text and be formed by it today. Biblical meaning is found in the way the church comes to understand the Bible more and more fully in its life, liturgy, and theology.

Those who wrote the books of the Bible gave to them their normative meaning, the original meaning that captured the essence of the tradition. The church gave new meaning to the texts as the canon was formed. The church continues to find meaning in its sacred books as they are the focal point of its ongoing life. While it is important to distinguish between what a biblical passage meant and what it means, these meanings are not unrelated or totally separable. The quest for meaning is open-ended, and it is the interaction of all these sources of meaning that makes biblical study so rich and exciting today.

Through its biblical scholarship, the community of faith today continues to do what its ancestors did with the biblical traditions. It makes them alive in new settings, new cultures, and new situations. It is the faith community that is both the carrier of tradition and the agent of creative reinterpretation. While any critic can interpret the Bible as literature, only the faithful community can interpret it as sacred and inspired Scripture.

CHAPTER TWELVE

How to Read and Study the Bible

When you began reading this book, you might have had a fear of reading the Bible. Maybe it seemed too overwhelming, too difficult, too confusing. Through the course of reading this book, perhaps some of those fears have begun to be sorted out and remedied. Hopefully your fears of the Bible have been replaced by awe for the Bible, by an understanding that the Bible can be a means of encountering our personal and loving God.

The real challenge, as you have certainly discovered, is making time for reading and studying the Bible and then actually doing it. But once daily Bible reading becomes a priority and regular part of our lives, the other choices come easily. What should I do with these few minutes I have set aside each day? Which books of the Bible do I read? Do I read a few pages each day, or a few verses? What do I do with passages I don't understand? Should I study the Bible alone or join a group to study with?

A Few Practical Suggestions

My first suggestion has to do with what books of the Bible to read. Do not start from page one of the Bible and start reading from cover to cover. Do not start with Genesis and think that you will read one book at a time until you have read the whole Bible. This is the most common way of approaching the Bible, a way you might have tried before, but the least common way to success. Most people read Genesis, then go on to Exodus, then begin to get bogged down with the ritual details and listings in Leviticus and Numbers, and soon give up in frustration.

Pick and choose from the library of books in the Bible. You might begin in the New Testament. Choose one of the gospels, maybe the gospel of the liturgical year, then read the Acts of the Apostles, the story of the early church. After that, choose a couple of letters from Paul's writings. Then after you become a bit familiar with the New Testament, begin to venture into the Old Testament. Start by reading the book of Exodus, the story of Israel's formation as a people. Then you could read one of the prophets, or perhaps begin the books of Samuel to study the beginnings of Israel as a nation. With this selective reading of one book at a time, your reading will seem much more manageable. Instead of seeing daily Bible study as an overwhelming task set before you, focusing on one book at a time will encourage you to enter personally into the world of the Bible.

The pace of our Bible reading will probably vary from day to day. Some days you will want to read a chapter or two, other days, just a few verses. As you read, be alert to the broad context of your reading and also the small details. Sometimes it is advisable to read through a whole book rather quickly in order to get an overview of it. At other times we should read very slowly, savoring and reflecting on only a few words at a time. When reading Paul's shorter captivity letters, for example, you might want to read the whole letter from beginning to end, as you would read any letter you receive in the mail. Then you will certainly want to go back and read more slowly, reflecting especially on those passages you took note of in your more rapid reading.

Another practical suggestion is to mark up your Bible as you read it. Many people find it helpful to highlight sections or underline certain verses or make notes in the margin. This can help you focus and remember what you read. It will also mark out certain passages for you to go back to later on for inspiration and further reflection. There is nothing irreverent about writing in your Bible. The most important use of the Bible is to transfer the word from the printed page to your mind and heart. Whatever helps you to do that pays tribute to the word of God.

My most important recommendation is to read Scripture prayerfully. Always begin and end your daily reading with quiet prayer. Just a few seconds of quiet, asking God to be with you through the Holy Spirit, will make a world of difference in your attitude when approaching

Scripture. Prayer places us consciously in the presence of God. It makes us aware that it is God who is communicating with us when we read the Scriptures. It helps us to put all the distractions of the day out of our minds so that we can truly listen with our mind and our heart to the word of God.

Tools for Studying the Bible

Beginning to understand the Bible requires both reading and study. The cultural and language differences between the biblical world and our world are just too great to understand it well with just a superficial reading. Yet that gap can be bridged in a number of ways. We have already discussed the helps available within various editions of the Bible, such as footnotes, cross-references, and introductions. Let's now look at a few other tools for studying the Bible.

- *Commentaries.* These helpful books are written by biblical scholars in order to share with the reader a summary of scholarly findings on individual biblical books. Usually the author will take each passage and explain something of its background, the situation in which it was written, and the meaning intended by its original author. Sometimes commentaries help the reader understand the fuller meanings of the passage and begin to apply it to contemporary life. These commentaries can be a great help when read along with the biblical books.

  There are lots of biblical commentaries available today. The best one-volume commentaries on the books of the Bible are *The New Jerome Biblical Commentary* (Prentice Hall) and *The International Bible Commentary* (Liturgical Press). An outstanding commentary series, written at the popular level for new students of the Bible, is the *New Collegeville Bible Commentary* (Liturgical Press). This is a multi-volume commentary on each individual book of the Bible. Other multi-volume commentaries, written for the more advanced reader, are the *Berit Olam* series on the Old Testament books and the *Sacra Pagina* series on the New Testament books (Liturgical Press).

- *Bible Dictionaries.* Another helpful reference tool for study is a Bible dictionary. This provides helpful information about specific topics, words, or themes in the Bible. If you come across a word in your reading that you want to know more about, where it came from or how it is used in other parts of the Bible, a Bible dictionary is the ideal help. A few recommended one-volume dictionaries are these: *Dictionary of the Bible*, by John L. McKenzie, *Eerdmans Dictionary of* the Bible, and *The HarperCollins Bible Dictionary*. The six-volume *Anchor Bible Dictionary* has more extensive articles for deeper research.

- *Concordance.* A concordance of the Bible lists all the places in the Bible where a given word is used. It can be helpful in several ways. For example, if you want to find other passages in the Bible where the word "covenant" appears in order to compare its usage throughout the Bible, just look up "covenant" and you will find the complete list. Or, if you recall a few words of a passage but don't remember where to find it in the Bible, just look up one of the words you know, then look for its chapter and verse in the concordance. Each concordance is keyed to a particular translation since different Bibles use different English words to translate the original texts.

- *Bible Atlas.* This is a useful help for making the places of the Bible come alive. Ancient maps found in a Bible atlas will allow you to follow the journey of Abraham, to trace the route of Moses through the desert, and to see the Promised Land in its various stages of biblical history. New Testament maps will allow you to see where Jesus traveled through Galilee and Judea, to imagine the city of Jerusalem with its high walls and great Temple, to trace the many journeys of Paul, and to see how the church expanded in its early decades. It is interesting to match up the cities and countries of the Bible with modern places today. A Bible atlas can help us make the connections between our world and the world of the Bible.

A Method for Personal Daily Study

When you have determined to make daily reading of the Bible a regular part of your life and have set a realistic time and place, some type of method is essential. A few simple steps to keep in mind will help guide you through your study.

The first step is always prayer. Begin by quieting yourself and putting all the distractions of the day out of your mind. Call on the Holy Spirit and realize that God is with you. Holding your Bible in your hands, offer a simple prayer from your heart, praying that God guide you to truly hear his voice as you read.

Now, opening the Bible to the book and passage you have chosen for reading, begin to read. Read slowly and thoughtfully. Sometimes it might even be helpful to read aloud. Don't worry about parts you don't understand. Read with the whole context of the passage in mind, realizing the setting and what you have read before this passage.

Next, mark the passages that stand out to you. Passages that seem particularly inspiring or memorable could be underlined. If there is a key word that seems to stand out or summarize the reading for you, circle it. If there is a part you do not understand, you might mark that with a question mark.

Now, read any helpful tools that you have chosen to accompany your reading. It might be a separate commentary; it might be the footnotes and cross-references from your Bible. These will expand your understanding of the passage and perhaps help clarify some difficult passages.

Now spend some time reflecting on the passage. Go back to the words or verses that stood out to you. Think about the passages in reference to your own life. Ask yourself if there is any particular lesson or meaning the passage suggests for you. Ask yourself if there is any particular word or idea that you want to carry with you from this reading.

Finally, take a moment to thank God for speaking to you this day. Ask God to help you take to heart what you have read, to keep in mind the message for you, and to put into life the word you have received.

These simple steps will help you derive the most benefit from your daily reading and will help you open up your life to the transforming power of God's word. This method will vary slightly with different types of biblical writing, and certainly you should adapt these steps to your own unique temperament and reading style.

When studying a section of the Bible, your task is not complete until you have considered these four basic questions: 1) *What does the Scripture passage say?* Read the passage slowly and carefully with attention to its words and phrases. 2) *What does the Scripture passage mean?* Commentaries, footnotes, or other helpful tools will be helpful to understand the meaning intended by the authors and what God wants to communicate by means of their words. 3) *What does the Scripture passage mean to me?* This question requires personal reflection on the passage. As we allow God's communication to become a personal word, we can apply the passage to our own lives, our relationships, and our faith. 4) *What am I going to do about it?* God's word to us always implies a challenge and requires a personal response. Reflecting on the personal meaning of a passage requires that we act on the challenges presented to us and respond to God's word in the concrete circumstances of our lives.

Group Study of the Bible

While personal Bible reading is an important part of our individual lives as Christians, studying the Bible with a group of people can be an especially enriching experience. The word of God is addressed primarily to the community of faith and only secondarily to us as private individuals.

The primary way that we proclaim, hear, and respond to God's word is in the liturgy of the church. In the liturgy of the word we listen to the word proclaimed and preached, and we respond to that word in worship and in action.

Another way that we can continue and build on that communal experience of God's word is through a Bible study group. There are a number of benefits in studying the Bible with a group of people. We benefit from the encouragement and enthusiasm of others as we seek to make the Bible a regular part of our lives. We benefit from the shared ideas and insights of other people. We have a sense of guidance and direction in studying the Bible through a regular program of reading and study. We begin to realize how Christian life can be shared more fully with others through prayer, shared experiences, and mutual support.

A good group study program will create a balance between study and personal application. A program that is totally scholarly and historical fails to deal with the essential links between the Bible and our daily lives. On the other hand, a program that deals only with personal application and ignores the scholarly commentary is in danger of becoming too individualistic and ungrounded.

Another important characteristic of a group study is the balance it creates between personal study and the group process. It is almost impossible to go very deeply in the Bible without making individual study a part of daily life. A good weekly group process builds on the individual learning that members of the group have accomplished on their own throughout the week. A group that doesn't expect any study from its members between the group sessions will become too focused on individual opinion, and its results will be too superficial.

Catholic group study of the Bible should include several elements. It should, first of all, encourage daily personal study on biblical texts and commentary. It should also encourage personal prayer and reflection on those texts. The group process should create a spiritual community that encourages and supports one another as well as shares scriptural insights. The process should encourage members to share their reflections on the meaning of the texts and the possible ways they could apply the text to their own life experiences. Finally, individual and group Scripture study should lead to prayer. With personal reflection and prayer, Scripture study becomes a dialogue between God and the reader, listening to

God and responding to God. In these ways, studying the Bible involves the whole person: the mind, the heart, and the behavior—what we think, feel, and do.

Catholics should never have to go outside their own parish communities to other churches to learn about the Bible. As the family album of the people of God, the Bible is a great treasure. By understanding its pages, we understand who we are as God's family. We better comprehend what it means to be a follower of Christ and a member of his church.

Let's Go Forward

I hope this introduction to studying Scripture has been a help to you in beginning to understand the riches of the Bible. I have attempted to respond to some of the questions most commonly asked by people being introduced to the study of the Bible. This brief introduction, however, is only a beginning. The Bible opens for us a lifetime of exploration and discovery.

St. Gregory said, "Find the heart of God in the word of God." The ultimate goal of studying the Bible is to know the heart of God. We should read the word of God as words addressed to God's people through the ages as well as words personally addressed to us. The Scriptures have the power to change our hearts and to transform our lives, as individuals and as Christ's church.

God's word is a living word. Respond to this initial introduction by making a personal commitment to making the Bible a more regular and central part of your life in Christ.